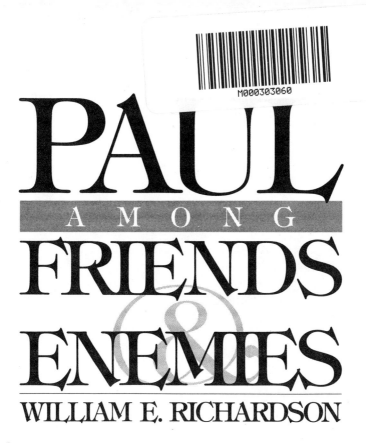

PAUL

AMONG

FRIENDS & ENEMIES

WILLIAM E. RICHARDSON

Pacific Press Publishing Association
Boise, Idaho
Oshawa, Ontario, Canada

Edited by Marvin Moore
Designed by Tim Larson
Cover illustration by John Steel
Typeset in 10/12 Bookman

Library of Congress Cataloging-in-Publication Data:

Richardson, William E., 1937-
    Paul among friends and enemies: a Bible reader's compan-
ion to the Pauline epistles / William E. Richardson.
       p.   cm.
    Includes bibliographical references.
    ISBN 0-8163-1084-X
    1. Bible. N.T. Epistles of Paul—Criticism, interpretation,
etc. 2. Bible. N.T. Acts—Criticism, interpretation, etc. 3. Paul,
the apostle, saint. I. Title.
BS2650.2.R49   1992
227'.06—dc20   91-40207
                                              CIP

92 93 94 95 96 · 5 4 3 2 1

Contents

DEDICATION

To Sandra,
without whose love and support extracurricular
work like this would be considerably more difficult.

Introduction

You are about to study one of the most exciting events in history—the explosive spread of Christianity in the midst of a hostile environment that should have doomed it from the start. Often, readers of history must look diligently for some rare incident of wit and humor to rescue them from the creeping paralysis of boredom. But the story of the formation of the apostolic church has its own flashes of color and interest built in. From the first formal nominating-committee meeting ("They put forward two men . . . and the lot fell to Matthias," Acts 1:23, 26, NASB), to the first violent disfellowshiping (which included the death sentence, 5:1-11), to the first divisive theological debate (15:1-20), the book of Acts reverberates with dynamic action. Of course, the purpose of this look at Acts is not merely to see all the action, but also to understand the historical setting for the study of Paul's epistles. In so doing, it is a considerable bonus that the material is interesting as well as informative.

While the radical expansion of the Christian church is graphically portrayed in the book of Acts, the development of its theology can only be found in the epistles. Thus it is the purpose of this book to introduce the reader to the book of Acts only as it will enhance our understanding of the Pauline epistles. Succeeding chapters will likewise include a careful look at the historical and thought contexts of each epistle. Such a study sounds heavy and uninteresting, but this is simply not the case. Paul's theology is interesting, at times even exciting, because it repeatedly emerges in lively inter-action with members. That is, he never sits down, pen in hand, saying, "Now I'm going to do some theological writing so Christians in all ages can better understand the nature of man in death." Instead, he gets word that the Thessalonian believers are grieving over the death of loved ones, so he reacts with extended encouragement about the "sleep" of death and the glorious reunion at the second advent. Thus the reason Paul's theology is not boring is that it is not "systematic"—it is not organized into subjects with all the supporting texts and logic carefully listed. He simply did not treat theological topics in isolation from real-life situations.

At this point, it is important to spell out a few of the principles of interpreting Scripture that have guided in the development of this book. First, many Bible-believing Christians speak confidently of "taking the Bible as it reads," implying that to "interpret" it is to somehow diminish it. When this method is used, no adaptation or accommodation of language is allowed. For example, Jesus' statement about casting away an offending eye or hand (Matt. 5:29, 30) will be interpreted to mean that thieves should lose their hands and those who lust should lose their eyes. Similarly, if Paul suggests that women should show their reverence in church by wearing a veil, this method would insist that women in any time and place should do likewise. A hat would not be adequate, since that is clearly an accommodation of the instruction. First-century veils were not at all like modern-day hats. But even the most "literalistic" interpreter makes some accommodation. It seems reasonable, then, that some adjustment has to be made for the time and place and culture in which the original language was used. But what safeguards are there against the danger of simply dismissing any unwelcome counsel as culturally conditioned and therefore irrelevant to "my situation"?

First, in view of the many authors and circumstances that are compiled in Scripture, any interpreter must look for the overall teaching of the Bible and not limit himself/herself to the apparent teaching of a very small passage. For example, Paul's statement in 1 Timothy 2:11 about women not teaching must be balanced by his comments elsewhere (e.g., Titus 2:3; 1 Tim. 5:14) that approve of certain types of women teachers. Similarly, his comment to Timothy about an apparent medicinal use of wine (1 Tim. 5:23) must be balanced by the many scriptural cautions given elsewhere against drinking.

Second, it is important to distinguish between a statement

of principle and the citing of a specific case or application. For example, when Paul wrote 1 Corinthians 11, the unchanging principle of reverence required women to wear long hair and veils and men to wear short hair and no hats. The principle of reverence remains, but the specific application has changed. Today, reverence in church is generally shown by conservative dress, quiet deportment, and no male head coverings. But it remains the responsibility of the interpreter to seek out the *principle* that lies behind the *specific case* which is being discussed. When this is not done, the Bible tends to become a giant rule book, wherein all the requirements are spelled out in concrete applications and no serious thought about unchanging principles is required.

Another important guideline is to consider carefully the historical context of the original writing. Since there is a considerable change of time, circumstance, and lifestyle between Paul's first-century readers and his twentieth-century readers, it is important that we do what we can to put ourselves back in the sandals of those who read him first. For only when our interpretation and application of instruction are informed by the original setting and meaning can we be protected from private, fanciful interpretations.

Perhaps the most difficult guideline of all is to accurately discern one's own place in history and how that might affect the application of Scripture. Even when the principle is determined, the way it is carried over into day-to-day living in the modern age sometimes requires careful thought. For example, in Galatians 3:28 Paul stated the principle of spiritual equality between Jew and Gentile, between master and slave, and between male and female. But social and political equality of these pairs was long in coming. The first pair, Jew/Gentile, was being brought into equality in Paul's day. But the master/slave and male/female problem had to await the leavening influence of the gospel upon society before significant social change took place. As the gospel seed grows, the consciousness of believers is awakened, first on one issue, then on another, but the precise moment when the church should take the initiative on a particular social issue can be difficult to determine.

Approaching Scripture with these guidelines takes a bit more effort than the more familiar devotional style of Bible reading, but the result will be a deeper knowledge of God's Word, which in turn will enable us to know Him better. And when we truly know Him, we will love Him and want to share what we know about Him.

While it is the design of this book to clarify and apply many New Testament passages, to save space, many of the Scripture texts are merely alluded to, not reproduced. Consequently, it would be helpful for the reader to have a Bible close at hand while reading this material.

Chapter
One

Acts—
Linking the
Gospels and the Epistles

Acts 1-12

"The times have changed" may be an old and worn-out phrase, but when people facing the twenty-first century read and apply instruction written in the first century, the old adage is still appropriate. With this in mind, plunging into a study of the Pauline epistles without giving some attention to the historical setting would be foolish. In the New Testament, that setting is found in the book of Acts. This book tells of Paul's conversion, of his temporary rebuff by the other apostles, of his first frustrating attempts at missionary outreach, and of his establishment of churches that later gave rise to his impassioned letter writing. Clearly the book of Acts is the natural link between the account of the "good news" in the Gospels and the clarification and dissemination of that same "good news" through Paul's letters to the early Christian communities.

The title

The title "The Acts of the Apostles" is slightly misleading as it suggests a historical account of the work of all the apostles. In actuality, the book focuses on only two apostles, Peter and Paul, and of these, only Peter was one of the original twelve. From the standpoint of content, the book might more accurately be called "Highlights in the Lives of Peter and Paul." However, in ancient times books often got titles from some word or phrase that occurred in the first few lines. Accordingly, since the book of Acts is a continuation of Luke's account of the "Acts" of Jesus (see Luke 1:1-4 and Acts 1:1, 2), it is fitting that his second volume be called "The Acts of the Apostles."

Authorship of Acts

The Lukan authorship of Acts is suggested by a comparison of Luke 1:1-4 with Acts 1:1-5, and it is also implied by the "we" sections in Acts. The simple change of pronouns from the third person (he, him, they) to the first-person plural (we, us) was probably not accidental. The casual manner in which the change is made, coupled with the author's excellent grammar throughout, suggests that he intended to switch pronouns. But scholars differ on the reasons for the change. Some have suggested that the "we" sections indicate a different author, while others speculate that at these points Luke simply incorporated the pronouns of the source he was using. But the content and style of the "we" passages are virtually indistinguishable from the rest of Acts, so different authorship is not likely. A better suggestion is that the use of "we" gives the stories a sense of immediacy, which makes them particularly compelling narratives. If that was Luke's intention, then it appears that on Paul's second missionary journey, Luke joined his group at Troas (16:8, "They went down to Troas;" 16:10, "We sought to go on into Macedonia"), traveled with them to Philippi, then stayed there while the group traveled on (16:40, "they . . . departed"). Later, Luke rejoined Paul on the third missionary trip when he passed through Philippi on his return to Troas (20:6). When this information is coupled with the fact that Luke is mentioned several times as a co-laborer with Paul (Col. 4:14; Philem. 23, 24; 2 Tim. 4:11) and is among those who sent greetings to the very communities they would have visited together, the close association of Paul with the author of Acts is apparent. In addition, the vocabulary, grammar, and style of writing are strikingly similar in Luke and Acts. Accordingly, the circumstantial evidence of Luke's authorship of Acts is very strong.

Organization of the book

While arbitrary divisions are often flawed, Acts does seem to have two primary concerns: the proclamation of the gospel to Jews by the ministry of Peter (1-12) and the gospel for Gentiles through the teaching of Paul (13-28). Of course, it is easily apparent that these divisions are not hard and fast. A prominent Gentile and his family are evangelized by Peter in chapter 10, and Paul is first introduced in chapter 7 and then more prominently in chapter 9. Furthermore, in the latter half of the book, Paul repeatedly approached Jews before preaching to Gentiles, even though it was his expressed ambition to proclaim the gospel to the Gentiles (Rom. 15:18). Nevertheless, there seems to be a shift in emphasis in chapter 13, as the focus moves from Jerusalem to Antioch, and the evangelistic teams, minus Peter, are sent out on extended trips to spread the gospel to the west.

Theme of the book

In Acts 1:8 the theme is sounded, not only for Acts, but also for the ministry and epistles of Paul: "You shall receive power when the Holy Spirit has come upon you; and you shall be my witnesses in Jerusalem and in all Judea and Samaria and to the end of the earth." This statement is both succinct and all-encompassing. Luke desired not simply to highlight the activities of two outstanding apostles, nor even to show the spread of Christianity, but along with these two to help the reader see the divine authority and power that made the whole incredible story possible. In time Paul came to feel that his entire world had been evangelized (Col. 1:23), and Luke must have had similar thoughts. Yet he would leave no doubt about the power that impelled them to action and brought about the results. Human effort alone could never accomplish it, but through the ministry of the Holy Spirit that same human effort could "[turn] the world upside down" (Acts 17:6). Thus, Luke's historical purpose was to show the rapid advance of the gospel, while his religious purpose was to call attention to the Holy Spirit as the driving force behind every significant development.

Place of origin

Though it is difficult to know with certainty the place of origin of Acts, there is some evidence that Luke was in Rome when he wrote the book. At least the abrupt conclusion in 28:31 suggests that the author was on the scene with Paul in Rome and cut off his account because there was nothing more to write. In addition, the book seems preoccupied, not only with showing the expansion of the church from Jerusalem to Rome, and hence to all his known world, but also to stress

> the favorable attitude of the Roman authorities to the first missionaries. His book is likely therefore to have close associations with the city which was both the seat of Roman government and also the place where ecclesiastical organization most rapidly took definite shape (G. H. C. MacGregor, "The Acts of the Apostles," in *The Interpreter's Bible*, ed. George A. Buttrick [Nashville: Abingdon, 1954], vol. 9, p. 22).

Luke's plan of presentation

Students of the book of Acts should bear in mind that behind Luke's historical document is a plan. Though it is a factual account, it is a selective history, carefully constructed so as to make a favorable impression on Luke's friend, Theophilus, who represented future Christians whose faith would need to be strengthened. Failure to keep this in mind often leads to preoccupation with historical precision, which is sometimes incidental to the author's intent. With this in mind, a surface analysis of the pre-Pauline section of Acts follows.

Acts 1-12—Observations and commentary

After a typical Greek introduction in which Luke reminds Theophilus of what he has already told him and announces what he is about to tell him (1:1-5), he records his version of Jesus' great commission to His apostles (1:8). In fact, verse 8 is actually the theme and organizational outline for the entire book. The scope of the commission must have seemed ambitious indeed, for to apostles just coaxed out of hiding, it would sound close to foolhardy to say that they would be witnesses "in Jerusalem and in all Judea and Samaria and to the end of the earth." But the encouraging thing about the Lord, when He sets before human beings a daunting challenge, is that He sooner or later sends the equipping power. So here, Jesus said, "You shall receive power when the Holy Spirit has come" (1:8). Similarly, in chapter 2:41 the church is born, three thousand strong, but only after spectacular demonstrations of the Spirit's power (see also 2:4-8, 11, 33, 37, 38). Luke proceeds with additional incidents that enhance the message of Spirit empowerment: the miracle in chapter 3:1-10, the ensuing arrest and release by the Jewish leaders in chapter 4, and the repetition of the same in chapter 5:12-42. The overwhelming impression gained is that the power behind all the action is divine ("the Holy Spirit said . . ." is the recurring phrase or idea). The story is fast-paced and seemingly out of human hands.

But the rapid growth is not unflawed. A historical account that includes "warts and all" is generally a more reliable record than one that presents it characters as unrealistically beautiful. The sad accounts of the devious Ananias and Sapphira in chapter 5 and of the whimpering Hellenists in chapter 6 show that the growing church was comprised of real flesh-and-blood people, not cold museum pieces. In addition, the incident with Ananias and Sapphira served as an important caution against the possible notion that membership in this group guaranteed healing from illness and an overall life of ease. After this event, no one motivated by greed or selfishness would dare to join the group (5:13).

In chapter 7:58 ("the witnesses laid down their garments at the feet of a young man named Saul"), Luke introduces

Paul into the narrative in an offhand manner that, by its very nonchalance, hints that more about him will follow. It is as if a spotlight has panned across a crowd and hesitated ever so briefly on the face of Paul. But the observer is left with the strong impression that the returning sweep will stop with Paul centered in the light. And while Peter holds center stage up to chapter 9 and appears again briefly in the Cornelius story in chapter 10, it seems that with the introduction of Paul, Luke has gotten to his central figure!

Over the years, the account of Paul's conversion (9:1-31) has come under intense scrutiny. Reactions have run the gamut from acceptance of Luke's account to total skepticism that a Pharisee could so quickly reverse himself. The disbelief has often centered on the suddenness of Paul's reversal and the apparently overwhelming power of God's Spirit. But the suddenness may have been more apparent than real. A conditioning process may have been going on in Paul's mind for some time. It is hardly accidental that Luke juxtaposed the dying testimony of Stephen ("Lord, do not hold this sin against them," 7:60) with the introduction of Saul as an eyewitness. As time passed, that selfless martyrdom burned itself into the fabric of Saul's being. When the voice along the road derailed his mission to Damascus, he spent still more time in intense contemplation (three days in Damascus [9:9] and three years in Arabia [Gal. 1:17, 18]). Hence it is probably incorrect to speak of Paul's conversion on the Damascus road. At that point he was dramatically confronted by God, but only after quiet reflection was he converted. No doubt his experience was a paradigm of the numberless conversions throughout Christian history that have *appeared* to be the result of divine thunderbolts, but a lightning flash has yet to produce a Christian. Such a display may be necessary to secure our attention, but Christianity takes hold of us only after we have had time to think and reflect meaningfully on the particular confrontation God's Spirit has put before us.

Whatever psychological preparations preceded this dramatic event, and whatever conclusions contemporary thinkers reach about Paul's mystical experience on the road to Damascus, there can be little doubt that he looked back upon this divine intervention as the cause of the change in the direction of his life. Years later, when he defended himself against a mob (Acts 22:6-16), and again before Agrippa (26:12-18), he recounted the Damascus-road experience in detail, thus reflecting the awe with which he looked upon that event. Though it is difficult to determine just how his Pharisaism prepared him to encounter Christ, it is not difficult to see how dramatically that confrontation affected him.

The importance of the Damascus-road experience may also be seen in that he is the only apostle about whom such a dramatic about-face is recorded. All the others came to experience faith and trust in Christ as a result of a gradual dawning of the light as they associated with Him and with one another. Perhaps in His wisdom, God saw the importance to future generations of Christians of showing how the preeminent New Testament theologian was dramatically humbled, and how, in a relatively short time, he could be changed from persecuting Pharisee to champion believer. If an enemy as implacable as Saul could come to have faith, then surely John Doe Skeptic can also be changed!

The precise chronology of events following Paul's conversion are not very clear. When Acts 9:19-30 and Galatians 1:15–2:2 are read side by side, the time of Paul's trip to Arabia and his acceptance by the apostles seems out of harmony. However, it is important to keep in mind that the purpose of each of these authors is quite different. In Galatians, which is Paul's own account, the genuineness of his apostleship was under attack, and since the mark of a true apostle was to be an eyewitness (Acts 1:21, 22), Paul felt constrained to stress both the uniqueness and the authenticity of his apostolic calling. He did this by showing his independence from the other apostles while at the same time stressing that he too had had an eyewitness experience with the Lord. In contrast, as Luke constructed his account for the newly believing Theophilus, apostolic harmony was important, so he condensed the account, passing quickly from the divine confrontation in Damascus to the reconciliation between Paul and the other apostles. Thus, if Luke knowingly omitted certain details that Paul included, he was not in any sense being dishonest. Rather, both men presented the story effectively for the differing circumstances each represented.

Additional readings on chapter 1

1. F. F. Bruce, *Commentary on the Book of the Acts*, vol. 5 of *The New International Commentary on the New Testament* (Grand Rapids, Mich.: Eerdmans, 1974).
2. Francis D. Nichol, ed., *SDA Bible Commentary* (Washington, D.C.: Review and Herald, 1980), vol. 6, pp. 119-132.
3. Ellen G. White, *The Acts of the Apostles* (Boise, Idaho: Pacific Press, 1911), pp. 112-187.
4. William Williman, "Acts," in *Interpretation, A Bible Commentary for Teaching and Preaching*, ed. James L. Mays (Atlanta, Ga.: John Knox Press, 1988).

Chapter
Two

Paul's Mission Begins

Acts 13-20

The first missionary outreach of the apostolic church was not a private enterprise urged on the group by one insightful individual. It was only at the insistence of the Holy Spirit that meaningful evangelism got under way. Luke was clearly aware of this, for he attributed every significant development to the urging or presence of the Spirit (see Acts 2:4; 4:3, 31; 5:3, 32; 8:29; 13:2). Nevertheless, in spite of the many indications from God that they were to reach out to all unbelievers, including non-Jews (such as the gift of tongues at Pentecost in chapter 2; Philip's connection with the Ethiopian in chapter 8; the conversion of Cornelius in chapter 10), the apostles continued to show considerable reticence about moving beyond their familiar circles. In fact, during the first decade after Jesus left them, the apostles gave little indication that the term *apostle* ("sent one") meant anything to them. Year after year, the territory touched by the gospel message remained essentially the same—the familiar regions of Judea and Galilee. The notion of the gospel being spread to the ends of the earth seemed ambitious indeed. But with the Spirit's call of Paul and Barnabas in chapter 13:2, outreach activities changed dramatically. The following decade saw the gospel story explode toward the west, permeating Asia Minor, Macedonia, Greece, and even Rome. All this was accomplished, not by a high-tech media blitz, but by the simple, heartfelt testimony of a small but committed missionary band, prodded out of their complacency by the Holy Spirit. With the passage of time, the scope of Jesus' words, "to the end of the earth" (1:8), began to seem almost possible. This chapter will highlight Paul's three missionary journeys and show how those journeys set the stage for the various letters that were later sent to the fledgling Christian communities.

The first missionary journey (13:2-14:28)

As the missionary outreach of the church is introduced in chapter 13:1-3, several important details stand out. First, the headquarters for this aspect of church work had moved from Jerusalem to Antioch. Perhaps this move, recorded rather casually in chapter 11:20-26, was a necessary step to enable both believers and unbelievers to shed the Jewish stamp that was so closely associated with Jerusalem. Also, as mentioned earlier, the force behind each new development was divine, not human—"the Holy Spirit said." Yet while the initiative came from above, the work force was human. Presumably, the Spirit could have actually done the work of proclamation, but chose instead to work through human instruments for the collective good of the church. In addition, a nucleus of believers stood united in support of the outreach. Accordingly, the laying on of hands probably imparted no new power or grace on the evangelists (notice John Mark's withdrawal in 13:13); rather, it put the human stamp of approval and support on the divine plan. By laying their hands on the missionaries before sending them off, the elders showed the unity of the two missionaries with the Antioch believers who stayed home.

As the team began its work, it is interesting to note that the name of Barnabas is consistently listed before the name of Saul/Paul. Given Luke's penchant for accuracy of detail, the order of the names in chapter 13:2 suggests that Barnabas was still looked upon as the leader of the evangelistic team, with Saul, the newcomer, still needing to prove himself in the eyes of the other Christians. Nevertheless, though Luke mentioned

Barnabas first, and though the first stop on the journey was Barnabas's homeland of Cyprus, Saul quickly assumed leadership of the group (13:9), and following the advance to Asia Minor, Luke referred to them as "Paul and his company." Apparently, Saul's prominence was not long in developing.

The origin of the itinerary of the first missionary journey is not clear. Inasmuch as Barnabas and Mark were both natives of Cyprus, the visit to the island seems a natural beginning. However, as the travel continued, it appears that the missionary thrust was toward Gentiles wherever they happened to be. Accordingly, the Hellenistic influences in the lives of all these early evangelists fitted them well for the work of contacting non-Jews. But Saul's background uniquely qualified him for the extensive witnessing he was beginning.

In Paul's world, Roman citizenship was a cherished asset. It was Paul's passport to distant lands, his charm against evil, his protection from Roman scourgings. When the Roman military commander spoke of having bought his citizenship, Paul sounded a note of quiet pride when he replied, "But I was born a citizen" (22:28).

Yet Roman citizenship was only one element of Paul's unwitting preparation for his calling. There was also the influence of his childhood home. Tarsus was a Greek city that breathed the very atmosphere of learning and surrounded the young Saul with the typical Hellenistic attitudes of inquisitiveness and love of education. The Greek fascination for logic and detail left its mark on the mind of one who would one day stand among the brightest philosophers and engage in verbal jousts that left them fascinated by Christianity, if not converted to it.

Finally, there was his training by Gamaliel, a Pharisee of such reputation that Paul later spoke with pride of being a "Pharisee of the Pharisees." Such Jewish roots gave Paul an understanding of, if not patience with, intransigent Jews, who vigorously opposed his Christian views.

In all, Paul's background was a singular equipping for his mission, which he could not possibly have anticipated. Surely no human visionary would have thought that the best person to send as the first Christian missionary was a staunch Pharisee with Roman citizenship who was fluent in Greek. If ever a person was unwittingly prepared for his/her role in life, it had to be Saul of Tarsus.

As the missionary travels progressed, they revealed Paul's single-minded purpose. His one concern was to share his gospel with the unenlightened wherever they were, and of course they were mostly in the cities. Consequently, Paul apparently spent little time in the country or even enjoying the beauties of the natural world. Some of the territory through which he traveled is unspeakably beautiful. The mountains of Greece, rising above the Aegean Sea, create vistas that are nothing short of inspirational. Yet Paul gave us no indication that he even noticed. In all his letters, there is not one hint that the loveliness of sea and sky made any impression upon him at all.

> His interests were in the spiritual improvement of the race and not in the enjoyment of material things. His world was the world of men, the world of spiritual conflicts, the world of sinning, sorrowing, struggling humanity, the world without salvation and in starving need of salvation from sin (D. A. Hayes, *Paul and His Epistles* [Grand Rapids, Mich.: Baker, 1969], p. 77).

Paul moved quickly from city to city, seeking the crowds, finding the masses, and preaching his theme: The crucified and risen Christ means no more works-righteousness and no more condemnation.

When one reads in chapters 13:4–14:28 the account of the first missionary journey, certain conclusions leap out. First, it is clear that Luke chose carefully the activities he wished to highlight. The events detailed and the speeches recorded were surely abridged editions, or "the world itself could not contain the books that would be written" (John 21:25).

Also, it is interesting how faithful Paul was to go "to the Jew first, and also to the Greek." Without fail, Paul's first concern upon entering a village was to seek out the local synagogue or an equivalent place of prayer. Only after the local Jews made clear their hostility to his message did he turn his efforts toward the Gentiles of the area. Throughout his ministry, this procedure varied little, even after he threw down what sounded like a final ultimatum. When, in the heat of exasperation, he thundered to the Antioch Jews, "Lo, we turn to the Gentiles" (13:46, KJV), it sounded truly final. But seven verses later he sought out the Iconium synagogue, and the cycle was repeated. While the Gentiles proved time and again to be the more responsive hearers, Paul could not bring himself to give up on his "kinsmen by race" (Rom. 9:3).

On the island of Cyprus, Luke highlighted only the events at Paphos. First was the conversion of the Roman official Sergius Paulus, juxtaposed with the harassment by his magician, Elymas. Luke probably included the mention of Elymas's Jewish background on purpose. In a wide variety of incidents, he cast the Jews in a poor light and the Romans in a favorable light. The events at Paphos comprised the first of many such portrayals. In this incident, the Roman became the first of all those non-Jews who listened and responded to the gospel invitation, while Elymas was the precursor of all those, Jews or Gentiles, who set themselves in opposition to the Christian message and its messengers. Elymas's complete discomfiture stood as a warning.

Luke chose this point to casually introduce Saul as "Paul." While various explanations for the name change have been suggested, it is likely that, having been born a Roman citizen, *Paul* was not an entirely new name.

In those days nearly all Jews had two names. One was a Jewish name, by which they were known in their own circle; the other was a Greek name, by which they were known in the wider world. Sometimes the Greek name translated the Hebrew. So Cephas is the Hebrew and Peter the Greek for a rock; Thomas is the Hebrew and Didymus the Greek for a twin. . . .

So Saul was also Paul. It may well be that from this time he so fully accepted his mission as the apostle to the Gentiles that he determined to use only his Gentile name. If so, it was the mark that from this time

he was launched on the career for which the Holy
Spirit had marked him out and that there was to be no
turning back (William Barclay, *The Acts of the Apostles*,
The Daily Study Bible Series [Philadelphia:
Westminster, 1976], p. 100).

At Perga the young John Mark turned back (13:13).
Whether that decision was the result of fear or immaturity is
unclear, but it was a decision he came to regret and one Paul
remembered and held against him. In Antioch of Pisidia Paul
spoke to the Jews, and Luke recorded the speech in considerable detail (13:16-41), no doubt as a sample of such
speeches that Paul would repeat many times. Elsewhere,
Luke recorded Paul's synagogue speeches in very abbreviated forms (see 17:3).

If this Antioch sermon is a sample of Paul's approach to his
fellow Jews, it is interesting to note that he started on
common ground to disarm hostility, thus preparing them to
listen to the harder part of his message. After a brief account
of God's intervention and deliverance in Old Testament
times, Paul linked Jesus to David, the Jews' perennial hero,
then moved at once to the heart of the gospel message.
Christ's death, ordered by Jews and carried out by Pilate, was
not a defeat but a triumph, for God raised Him from the tomb,
and all this was a fulfillment of Old Testament prophecy.
Furthermore, this death and resurrection made possible the
forgiveness of sins, which heretofore was impossible under
the laws of Moses. Finally, all was for naught unless the
gospel was personally believed and accepted.

Just as this Antioch sermon was given as an example of
Paul's many succeeding synagogue speeches, so the re-
sponse that followed was typical of what would often be
repeated—many believed, jealous Jews became enraged,
Paul was expelled or physically abused, and he sought out
Gentiles, who were more responsive.

In Lystra, in the midst of a mostly pagan audience, events
revolved around a miracle of healing (14:8-18). The miracle
so excited the crowd that a tumultuous demonstration of
adulation for the apostles got a bit out of hand, and when

some unhappy Jews from Antioch and Iconium showed up, the demonstration turned ugly. In fact, without divine intervention, Paul might well have died in Lystra.

The Jerusalem Council (Acts 15:1-35)

Successful evangelism sometimes sharpens the focus on the internal flaws of a church. To put it another way, new blood may cause a violent reaction. The events surrounding the Jerusalem Council can be described as the sluggish reactions of the orthodox to the exciting results of sweeping evangelism. The outcome of the debate was crucial to the continued expansion of Christianity. By their successful preaching to people of pagan background, Paul and his group inadvertently forced the issue of which ritual practices the Christian church would require of its believers. Until now, the Jewish-Christian leaders assumed that all Christians would be Jewish Christians. As they understood it, the Christ story was an addition to Judaism. The idea that the old wineskins of Judaism could not contain the new wine of Christianity had not caught hold. But with the influx of numerous Gentile converts, a great doctrinal issue had to be resolved: Would circumcision and the temple rituals be required of all believers? The Christians still headquartered in Jerusalem said Yes, while those of Antioch, taking a more liberal view, said No. The result was the first serious theological rift in the church, and it needed swift and clear resolution. After vigorous debate, the conference concluded that circumcision and a few other Jewish rituals must not be required of Gentile converts. However, certain concessions could be made without weakening Christian principle that would help to pacify those with strong Jewish roots.

Therefore, without compromising the Gentiles' Christian liberty, James gave it as his considered opinion that they should be asked to respect their Jewish brethren's scruples by avoiding meat which had idolatrous associations or from which the blood had not been properly drained, and by conforming to the high Jewish code of relations between the sexes instead of remaining content with the lower pagan standards to which they had been accustomed. This would smooth the path of social and table fellowship between Christians of Jewish and Gentile birth (F. F. Bruce, *The Book of the Acts*, p. 311).

As a result of this decisive meeting, the fledgling church was set free from what would surely have been a serious impediment to Christian expansion among the Gentiles.

This council helped people see that Christianity was not simply an offshoot or subgroup of Judaism but was also an approach to God through faith in Christ that was free, not only from ritual circumcision, but also from the limiting notion that Christianity was just an up-to-date form of Judaism.

The second missionary journey (Acts 15:36–18:22)

The second missionary trip began just off-key with Paul and Barnabas vigorously disagreeing about the value of John Mark for their mission. Paul looked upon Mark's earlier wavering as a flaw of sufficient magnitude to disqualify him for another trip. Barnabas, on the other hand, was considerably more tolerant and wanted to give his young cousin another chance. The fact that Luke did not gloss over this bit of strife is a testimony to his honesty and accuracy, especially since he did not suggest that Paul was right and Barnabas wrong.

When the journey actually began, Barnabas and Mark sailed back to Cyprus and virtually disappeared from the New Testament record. Paul and his new companion, Silas, continued in focus as they visited some of the Galatian communities that Paul had visited on the first trip. At Lystra they met Timothy and made him a member of the team but not until he had been circumcised. At first reading, this action seems to contradict the very thing Paul had fought to win at the recent Jerusalem Council. But this was one of those situations in which Paul's pragmatism, coupled with his sense of mission, led him to take a middle position. Although Timothy's Greek father caused him to be thought of as Gentile and thereby free of the need for circumcision, his Jewish mother raised some uncertainty about his actual status. Because Paul and his team would be having close contact with so many Jews, and since the issue at stake was not considered a requirement for salvation, Paul apparently saw no inconsistency between his action here and the conclusion of the Jerusalem Council. Since no principle would be compromised, Paul preferred to take an action that would disarm criticism and possibly open doors for evangelism that might otherwise remain closed. This was one of those times when he felt he could be "all things to all men, that I might by all means save some" (1 Cor. 9:22). Later, when he refused to allow Titus to be circumcised (Gal. 2:3), the issue was very different. Titus was a full-blooded Gentile, and thus was an example of those liberated by the Jerusalem Council. Furthermore, Titus's circumcision was being urged by the Judaizing Christians as a necessity for salvation, which was just what the Jerusalem Council had concluded was unnecessary.

At Philippi, Luke recorded three incidents that revealed the power of the gospel to change different kinds of lives. First was the faithful Jewish woman named Lydia, who, with her family, believed and was baptized. Next, the demon-possessed slave girl was delivered. Finally, amidst the upheaval and trauma of an earthquake, the hardened jailer was converted (16:11-34). In addition to giving the historical facts, Luke seems to be saying, "If such diverse lives as these can be changed, surely the incredible power of the gospel is evident."

Paul's stay in Thessalonica was relatively short (17:1-9), and yet it was a community to which he later sent two epistles. Perhaps one reason he wrote those epistles was that his stay was long enough to form a nucleus of believers but not long enough to clarify certain theological concerns. Due to his hasty exit from Thessalonica and his concern that the fledgling church be better established, Paul had Timothy and Silas remain in the area to further establish the work and then bring him word. It appears from Acts 17:10, 14, 15 and 18:1, 5 that after Paul fled Thessalonica, he traveled south, making brief stops in Berea and Athens before settling in for a longer stay in Corinth. There, after a number of weeks, he was reunited with his co-workers, who brought him good news about the progress of the work in Thessalonica. He responded to that report by sending off a letter to the believers there, making 1 Thessalonians his earliest epistle.

Paul's stay in Athens was probably disappointing to him in that the converts were so few (17:34) and the reaction of the philosophers so negative (17:32). In contrast, his ministry in nearby Corinth was much more rewarding. Although some of the usual harassments continued, he stayed there more than a year and a half (18:11, 18), and his subsequent letters indicate that a sizable Christian community was established.

The third missionary journey (18:23–21:17)

Luke showed little interest in the traveling part of this third journey, choosing rather to concentrate on Paul's three-year stay in Ephesus and his three-month stay in Corinth. Accordingly, he collapsed scores of miles and many weeks into the sweeping phrase, "Paul passed through the upper country and came to Ephesus" (19:1). Even much of the time Paul spent in the two major cities Luke quickly summarized by his condensing statement in 19:10 that, as a result of Paul's two years of preaching in Ephesus, "all the residents of Asia heard the word of the Lord." While that may be slightly overstated, his Ephesian ministry was important for the spread of the gospel through Asia. No doubt the seven churches of Revelation were conceived and nurtured into existence as a result of Paul's evangelistic activities in Ephesus at this time. While he was in Ephesus, Paul not only spawned new churches; he also maintained interest and contact with old ones like Corinth. There is little question that it was during his Ephesian visit, on his third journey, that Paul wrote 1 Corinthians. Later, he traveled a northern loop that took him back to Corinth, and somewhere en route he wrote his second letter to the Corinthians.

Luke's chronological details are not very precise, for in chapter 19:21 he indicates that time has gone by but gives no clue as to how much time. Similarly, in verse 23 he adds, "about that time," but sheds little light on when, during the Ephesian ministry, "that time" was. However, the length of the Ephesian ministry is specifically stated to have been at least three years (20:31)—the longest Paul ever stayed in any city on his travels. During this sojourn, perhaps near the end of his stay in Ephesus, one of the primary events was a noisy demonstration for the goddess Artemis that was orchestrated by mercenary-minded Demetrius, a silversmith. Luke seems to include this incident to give one more example of the futility of opposing those who have aligned themselves with the Lord and His cause. The story ends with the embarrassing dismissal of the demonstrators by one of their own officials (19:40, 41).

In Acts 20:1, 2 we see again just how selective Luke was regarding what he related and what he passed over. Here, in the space of only two verses, Paul traveled from Ephesus around the northern loop to Corinth, no doubt a trip of several months. He remained in Corinth for three months (20:3), during which time he wrote Romans and possibly Galatians.

Paul's return from his third missionary foray generated considerably more detail and comment than his trip out. It appears that Paul timed his return so that he could be in Jerusalem in time to celebrate the Passover. However, just before he departed from Corinth, a death threat leaked out (see Acts 20:3), so he quickly changed plans. Perhaps he was to be murdered on board the ship. In any case, his sudden change of travel plans foiled the attempt but necessitated a much longer return trip. Instead of sailing straight across the Aegean Sea, he took a northern route by land that must have lengthened his trip by several weeks.

At the same time, the altered itinerary enabled Luke to rejoin the team. At least his pronouns imply as much, for when the group passed through Philippi, it is suddenly "we" instead of "he" ("*we* sailed away from Philippi," 20:6).

On the return trip, Luke highlighted events at just two stops, one in Troas and one in Miletus. At Troas the church held an evening farewell meeting with Paul so he could give them his last loving instructions. He must have had many such meetings as he traveled, but Luke records this one because of the miraculous incident with Eutychus. Some have seen in this passage (20:7, 8) an argument for Sunday worship, but the time of the meeting seems too incidental to provide proof of a divine decree about a worship day. It was probably held in the evening because the believers were working-class people who could not meet during the day, and it was held that particular evening, "not because it was Sunday, but because Paul was ready to depart" (*SDA Bible Commentary*, vol. 6, p. 387).

The final stop of importance on this return trip was at the port city of Miletus. This city was only a few miles south of Ephesus, but apparently it provided the most convenient harbor for a brief stop. Paul's desire to attend Passover having been frustrated, he now hoped to make it to Jerusalem for the Pentecost festival (20:16), so time was of the essence. Still, he wanted one more meeting with the Ephesian believers, whom he had come to love during his three-year stay among them. So he sent word and had them meet him in Miletus. With eyewitness detail Luke records the tenderness and pathos of that farewell address (20:18-38), which is the only example he gives of a Pauline speech to a solely Christian audience. It contains an interesting mix of exhortations and reminiscences, ending in that emotional scene made especially poignant because of Paul's conviction that "they should see his face no more" (20:38).

Paul's final visit to Jerusalem was marked with pathos and turbulence. When it seemed clear that trouble awaited him (21:10, 11), friends pleaded with him to not go, but his determination was unswerving (21:13). The reasoning of the James party that Paul should go through a cleansing ritual and thereby defuse some radical criticism (21:18-25) ultimately drew him into a whirlpool of events from which he was unable to free himself. In spite of the conclusions of the Jerusalem Council, a rift had continued between Christians of Jewish and Gentile background. Still, James's efforts can be viewed as an attempt to pull the factions into close harmony and thereby make possible the advance of the church.

The first mob scene developed when Jews from Asia, probably visiting Jerusalem for Pentecost, saw Paul in the temple and falsely charged him with defiling the temple with Gentiles. He was saved from certain death (21:31) by a Roman military commander who allowed him to give a speech of defense to the Jews who had attacked him. Paul wisely stressed his own Jewish roots, and all went well until he favorably mentioned the Gentiles (22:21), whereupon pandemonium again erupted. The next day a more orderly hearing with the Jewish leadership convened, only to dissolve into chaos when Paul pitted Sadducee against Pharisee over the resurrection issue (23:6-10). When a plot against his life was revealed (23:12-16), Paul was moved to Caesarea, where his case was stalemated for two years (24:27). When the Roman governor Felix was replaced by Festus, Jewish pressure caused Festus to reopen the case against Paul, which the governor readily saw was no case at all. Paul was given the opportunity of being tried in Jerusalem, whereupon he appealed his case to Caesar in the belief that his life was valued more by the Romans than by the Jews. Subsequently, Festus solicited help from Herod Agrippa II to draft a reasonable charge against Paul to send with him to Rome (25:24-27), but after hearing Paul's defense, both officials admitted his innocence (26:31). However, Paul's appeal to Caesar had to be honored, so he was sent to Rome, where, probably because the charge against him was so unclear, his case was left in limbo for at least two more years. At this point (about A.D. 63) Luke's account comes to an end with Paul under a kind of house arrest, but allowed to teach and write with a certain amount of freedom. Luke does not record the later ministry and death of Paul because at the time he finished this writing, they had not yet taken place.

Additional readings on chapter 2

1. William Barclay, *The Acts of the Apostles*, The Daily Study Bible Series (Philadelphia: Westminster, 1976).
2. F. F. Bruce, *Commentary on the Book of the Acts*, vol. 5 of The New International Commentary (Grand Rapids, Mich.: 1974).
3. Ellen G. White, *The Acts of the Apostles*, pp. 188-220; 231-242; 281-297.

Chapter

Three

The First Epistles
1 and 2 Thessalonians

Have you ever written to a friend or relative and then remarked that it had turned out to be "quite an epistle"? If so, what did you mean? Was the letter unusually long or serious or religious? The statement does imply some sort of distinction between "letters" and "epistles."

First, a letter is usually written to an individual or group with only their situation in mind. There is no thought of permanence or of continuing application of the contents in other settings. No thought of posterity or publication comes to the mind of the author. Second, since the author and the recipients are normally well known to each other, a letter tends toward informality and uses terms of intimacy or frankness. In addition, most letters are of an occasional nature, having little formal organization.

In contrast, an epistle is a conscious literary endeavor with at least some thought given to distribution or publication. Since it is usually written to more than one individual, the terms used tend to be less familiar, more general, and more polished. Furthermore, the thoughts are more ordered and systematized than is true of most letters.

Given such definitions, it is nevertheless difficult to categorize the letters of Paul. Some of them have the occasional, informal tone of a letter, while others have the feel of a universally applicable epistle. Thus the little letter to Philemon seems addressed only to a personal friend about a particular situation, whereas the treatise called Romans seems clearly to be an epistle of universal appeal. At the same time, there are personal elements in Romans 16 and universal aspects in the personal letters to Timothy. Consequently, because the lines of distinction cannot be drawn with surgical precision, scholars have continued to use both "epistle" and "letter" to describe the Pauline correspondence. Nevertheless, it is helpful to keep in mind the definitions given above.

One helpful classification of Paul's letters, given by Everett Harrison, is both chronological and topical. He suggests they divide

> chronologically into the Eschatological, which belong to the second missionary journey (I, II Thessalonians); the Soteriological, written during the third missionary journey (Galatians, I and II Corinthians, Romans); the Imprisonment or Ecclesiological emanating from the first Roman imprisonment (Ephesians, Colossians, Philemon, Philippians); and the Pastoral (I Timothy and Titus during a period of release, II Timothy from the second Roman imprisonment) (Everett F. Harrison, *Introduction to the New Testament*, rev. ed. [Grand Rapids, Mich.: Eerdmans, 1977], p. 259).

Paul's style

While they vary somewhat from one another in content, Paul's letters all have a style and vocabulary that strongly suggest a common authorship. Each one begins with a greeting, which usually includes a word of thanksgiving for the believers' progress in the faith. This is followed by a doctrinal section, which is often followed by some practical exhortation. Finally, Paul often sent some personal messages, ending with a brief autograph in his own hand. However, Paul was a free spirit and varied this format if it seemed to slow down the rapid flow of his thought. Thus, when he wrote to the Galatians, he was so anxious to correct their mistaken ideas he didn't take time to thank them for their progress in the faith—perhaps because their progress was in the wrong direction. In fact, one of the outstanding marks of Paul's style is his apparent rush to get his thoughts on paper and before the eyes of the intended readers. Consequently, his is not the classic, polished style of Luke, but rather the rugged, broken, almost careless style of a man in a hurry, a man with much to say and too little time or space in which to say it. No doubt he could have composed sedate, well-ordered literary masterpieces, but he was too preoccupied with the urgency of his message to make sure that his rhetoric was nicely polished.

Accordingly, a common characteristic of Paul's epistles is the anacoluthon—a sudden interruption in the flow of his thought in order to give an extended parenthetical explanation. Usually the interruption is triggered by some word or idea that he feels needs immediate amplification. For example, in Romans 3:1, 2 he seems about to list some of the advantages of being a Jew, but after mentioning only the "oracles of God," he raises the issue of the unfaithfulness of some Jews and immediately attempts to show how their unfaithfulness in no way implicates God. He gets so involved in that line of reasoning that he doesn't come back to his original idea about the advantages of the Jews until chapter 9:1-5. It is probably the longest anacoluthon in Scripture. It is also typical of Paul's impetuous style of writing.

1 Thessalonians

Acts 17:1-9 gives Luke's description of the founding of the Thessalonian community of Christians. It was Paul's first visit to Thessalonica, and though brought to a boisterous and premature conclusion, it was strikingly successful, in that a very short visit resulted in a vibrant, growing church (1 Thess. 1:2, 3). The length of his stay, however, is not completely clear. The reference to "three sabbaths" (Acts 17:2, NASB) in the synagogue may well have been lengthened by a continuing ministry headquartered in Jason's house. This would explain why the Jews attacked Jason in their attempt to seize Paul (5). Also, Paul's reference to his diligent labor "night and day" (1 Thess. 2:9) while he was with them fits more easily into a ministry of several weeks than one of less than a month. Nevertheless, in a relatively short time, some Jews were converted, and "a great many . . . Greeks and not a few of the leading women" (Acts 17:4). Furthermore, the charge that they had "turned the world upside down" (Acts 17:6) must have had some substance in fact—in other words, the number of converts was rapidly increasing.

Authenticity of the letter

Both in 1:1 and 2:18, this short letter asserts that it is coming from Paul. Also, his two associates, Silas and Timothy, are known from Acts to have been with Paul on his second missionary trip, the time when the Thessalonian church was established. The subject matter—the fate of believers who die before the advent—argues for an early date, and that suggests it must have come from the hand of Paul, for who would have dared to distribute such a letter in his name while he was traveling from church to church and able to denounce any spurious use of his name. Also, the language of 4:15 implies that Paul believed he would witness the advent ("we who are alive") and, "It is difficult to think of anyone writing after Paul's death putting forth in Paul's name a statement that might be understood as meaning that the *Parousia* would take place during the Apostle's lifetime" (Leon Morris, *The First and Second Epistles to the Thessalonians*, vol. 20 of *The New International Commentary of the New Testament*, ed. F. F. Bruce [Grand Rapids, Mich.: Eerdmans, 1959], p. 27).

Occasion of the letter

Paul's abrupt departure from Thessalonica (Acts 17:8-10) may have lent itself to the problem that comes to focus in 1 Thessalonians. Apparently Paul had not thoroughly explained certain details regarding the nature and time of the second coming of Jesus. Consequently, as time went by and the Lord did not return, questions arose. Those questions Paul addressed in this, his first known letter.

At the time of this writing, Paul was in Corinth in the midst of his second missionary journey. He had earlier departed Thessalonica in a rush and was disturbed that the believers were hardly grounded in the faith. So, from Athens, he had sent Timothy back to Thessalonica to check on their progress and then bring him word (3:1-5). Now both Timothy and Silas had returned, and Paul was delighted to hear that the church was progressing nicely (1:2-10).

Date of the letter

Of course, these developments, together with the contents of 1 Thessalonians, indicate that considerable time had elapsed since Paul left that city. There had to be time for Timothy to make the trip from Athens to Thessalonica, spend time with the members, and then travel to Corinth. Also, it is apparent that several deaths had occurred in the church since Paul left (4:13). Finally, there had to be time for missionary fervor to develop and become known throughout Macedonia and Achaia (1:8). Since Paul was anxious to get word from the Thessalonians and just as anxious to let them know that he had indeed received their good news, this first letter to them was probably written during the early weeks or months of his eighteen-month stay in Corinth (Acts 18:11), or sometime in the year A.D. 51, the earliest of Paul's known documents.

Observations and commentary

The letter begins with the greeting that Paul used consistently in his letter writing—"grace to you and peace." His term *grace* is not identical to the common term of greeting among the Greeks (they said *chairein*, he said *charis*), but it is clearly intended to sound similar and thus have a special attraction to those with Greek backgrounds. In a similar way, *peace* was the common greeting among Hebrews. Thus, in this very simple greeting, Paul appealed to the two groups that predominated in his audiences, Greeks and Hebrews.

Since Paul and his team had been treated so shamefully in Thessalonica (Acts 17:5-9), it is reasonable to conclude that the growing church in that city would likewise suffer the slings and arrows of the enemies. It is no surprise, then, that one of Paul's aims in his letters to them was to encourage them in the face of continuing opposition. Accordingly, he began his letter with words of praise and thanksgiving, thereby encouraging the members to persevere (1:2-10). Also, Paul's frequent references to his own hardships were no doubt intended to serve as encouragement—inasmuch as he had endured, so could they (2:9-12; 3:7-10).

Even though Acts 17:4 states that some of the Jews in Thessalonica were converted, most of the Thessalonian Christians probably came directly out of heathenism. Judaism at this time was not infected with idol worship, so when 1 Thessalonians 1:9 says, "You turned to God from idols," their pagan background is obvious. Accordingly, though Paul's language is often interspersed with Old Testament expressions, he makes no direct appeal in the Thessalonian letters to the Old Testament as a final authority. Clearly, the Thessalonians came largely from Gentile backgrounds.

As you read through the letter, Paul's primary concern is clear. Though the chapters vary in approach and content, each one concludes on the same note—the coming of the Lord. In 1:10 he admonishes them to "wait for his Son from heaven." At the end of chapter 2, Paul tells his hearers that they will be his "crown of boasting" at the coming of the Lord. In 3:13 he hopes that they will be holy at the "coming of our Lord Jesus," and 4:15-18 includes a very specific and picturesque portrayal of the Lord descending from heaven with a shout and a trumpet blast. It is one of the most colorful pictures of that event to be found in Scripture. Then, in his conclusion of the letter, he makes one more reference to the coming of the Lord.

In this vein, it is interesting to note that the Greek term *parousia* is used twenty-four times throughout the New Testament, and seven of those occurrences are in these short letters to the Thessalonians. Literally, the word meant "coming" or "appearance," but was commonly used to describe the arrival of an important dignitary. In early Christian literature it took on the technical sense of a royal visit. It seemed to especially emphasize the idea of the "presence" of the Lord with His people. In 1 Thessalonians 2:19, a portion of the earliest Christian literature we have, Paul refers to the glorious return of the Lord. In ancient times people were occasionally expected to show their respect by providing a crown for a visiting king, but here Paul suggests that the Christians themselves will be their Lord's crown.

Though Paul vigorously teaches the imminent return of the Lord, it is significant that he also shows the need of working while waiting. Accordingly, his own example of financial independence (2:9-12) was designed to encourage them to be like-minded. He states it explicitly in 4:11, 12, though not with the vigor he later used in 2 Thessalonians, when the problem of idle waiting had become much worse.

The strong pastoral attachment Paul had for his children in the faith is readily apparent in his language in 3:5-10. His anguish over not knowing whether the "tempter had tempted" them could only arise out of a genuine compassion like that between parents and children. It follows that such intense personal concern would give rise to practical ethical exhortation, which Paul spelled out in 3:11–4:12 and again in 5:14-22. While his ethical and behavioral expectations were high, Paul made it clear that only Christ could provide the power to "establish your hearts" (3:13). Determination to behave well is never sufficient motive or power to enable a person to be really successful at living the Christian life.

In chapter 4 Paul continued his instruction on practical Christian living, and in verse 4 he made an unusual reference to the believer taking for himself a "*vessel*" (KJV) in sanctification and honor. Although a common interpretation is that Paul had in mind the judicious selection of a wife (see the RSV), he rarely used the term *vessel* in that way. Furthermore, such a term for wife is not particularly noble, yet Paul consistently set forth a high view of marriage. Thus, another view of this text concludes that Paul here used *vessel* to refer to each man's body, and is thus suggesting that the Thessalonians should keep their bodies pure. In either case, the stress on morality and holy living is clear.

From the conclusion of chapter 4 and the beginning of chapter 5 it is clear that the Thessalonians were perplexed about the timing of the second advent of Christ, particularly as that event had to do with the death of some of their loved ones. They seemed to think that unless they lived to see the advent, the separation of death would be permanent. But Paul gently chided them for grieving just like "others . . . who have no hope" (4:13). It is the certainty of Christ's resurrection that ensures the resurrection of their sleeping loved ones and the resultant glorious reunion. Thus, when Paul said that "God will bring with him those who have fallen asleep," he no doubt had in mind Christ bringing with Him from the grave all those who had fallen asleep as believers. The reunion thus guaranteed (4:17), Paul added that this was a message of comfort for all concerned.

He then reassured them in another way—the coming day need not surprise them and catch them unprepared. While he used the ominous figure of the "thief in the night," he assured them that that figure only pertained to "night people," which the Thessalonian believers were not. Rather, they were "sons of light and sons of the day," so they had nothing to fear, though sloth and indifference were always to be guarded against. In any case, the message that begins with the fearful-sounding "thief" figure ends with the hopeful message, "Encourage one another and build one another up," and "be at peace among yourselves" (5:11, 13). Apparently, the advent is not meant to strike terror to Christian hearts, but only to rebellious ones, who live in the same darkness that hides thieves.

2 Thessalonians

According to Acts 18:11, on his second missionary journey, Paul stayed in Corinth for a year and a half. As mentioned above, it was there that he first got word of the Thessalonian progress and promptly sent off the first letter. Since both Thessalonian letters begin with the same greeting from the same three persons, it is reasonable to conclude that the historical setting of the two letters is essentially the same. Between the writing of the two letters, sufficient time was needed for the first letter to be delivered and word of its reception and the ensuing response to get back to Paul. In other words, the two letters were probably written within a few weeks of each other, in A.D. 51/52.

Authenticity of the letter

The authenticity of the second letter to the Thessalonians is tightly linked to that of the first letter. The language and theology of both letters is clearly Pauline, and from early in the second and third century, this second letter was tied to Paul and to the first letter.

Occasion of the letter

Early in 2 Thessalonians the evidence jumps off the page that Paul's first letter had been eminently successful—too successful. Urgency for the advent had turned into a fetish. Excitement can bring dynamic, productive activity, but it can also bring counterproductive preoccupation. Unfortunately, the latter was the case with the Thessalonians. Now they were so worked up that they believed wild rumors, purportedly originating with Paul (2:2), that the day of the Lord "has come" (the word thus translated can also be rendered "is come," or "is at hand"). Apparently, the community had fallen into a misguided, overworked enthusiasm, which Paul saw would be detrimental to their long-term spiritual experience. So now he worked to counteract some of the overzealous reactions to his first letter.

Observations and commentary

After his typical greeting and giving thanks to God for the vibrant faith of the Thessalonians, Paul encouraged them to stand firm in the face of suffering because God would soon right all such wrongs when the Lord Jesus "is revealed from heaven with his mighty angels in flaming fire" (1:7). This introduction moved Paul into the primary concern of the letter, which was the timing of the great day of the Lord. After his earlier graphic description of the advent in 1 Thessalonians 4:13-18, the believers had concluded that the moment had virtually arrived. Now, in the second chapter of his second letter, Paul had to readjust their timetable. Before the great day can come, there must first be a notorious rebellion during which a sinister evil power will be revealed. This power will be characterized by blasphemous claims (4), a lawless attitude (8), supernatural power, and close association with Satan (9). It will also be characterized by a certain mystery— a mystery that Paul's description did not resolve. He spoke of the power as already at work in his time (7) but added that the being who personifies that power will be destroyed by the brightness of the Lord's appearing. At this point Paul sounds like an apocalyptic writer on the order of John the revelator, using colorful symbols and metaphors rather than straight-forward speech—and nothing seems to pique the curiosity of Bible interpreters quite like symbolic, metaphoric language. Such passages are usually subject to a wide variety of inter-pretations, and this passage is no exception. From early years expositors have speculated about what power Paul had in mind and when it will be revealed.

One common interpretation holds that the papacy is the power which best fits the various descriptive terms used by Paul (Leon Morris, *The First and Second Epistles to the Thessalonians*, pp. 220, 221). And even though Paul said the mystery of lawlessness was "already at work," long before the papacy existed as an organized entity, this view holds that the lawless spirit which later pervaded some of the papal regimes was developing even in Paul's day.

Another theory suggests that he referred to an emperor or emperors in his own day, for some of the Caesars were truly blasphemous in their claims and were certainly "already at work." This view is weakened, however, by the suggestion that the power described will have a final manifestation in the end time that will result in its being slain by "the breath of his mouth" and "by his appearing and his coming" (8).

It seems more reasonable to conclude that Paul had a larger, cosmic picture in view. The ultimate hostile power, the one Paul elsewhere called the "enemy" (1 Tim. 5:14), was Satan. But the "man of lawlessness" may take on other names and other faces. It is always the "activity of Satan" (9), but not always the person of Satan, that is visible. Through-out much of Paul's ministry, the Roman government was a positive influence on his missionary party, occasionally saving him from the mayhem intended by his enemies. At such times, Paul would be loathe to refer to the Roman officials as the "son[s] of perdition" (3). But as Revelation 18 points out, the time would come when no metaphor was quite strong enough to portray the vile nature of pagan Rome.

So also, while the papacy has had its sincere believers, it has also had popes, concerning whom the phrase "son of perdition" seems almost complimentary. For example, John XII, elected when he was only eighteen, was not known for his spiritual leadership. In fact, contemporary reports agree about his "disinterest in spiritual things, addiction to boorish pleasures, and uninhibitedly debauched life. Gossipy tongues accused him of turning the Lateran palace into a brothel" (J. N. D. Kelly, *The Oxford Dictionary of Popes* [New York: Oxford University Press, 1986], p. 126). When he was only twenty he died of a stroke he suffered, allegedly, while in bed with a married woman. The tales of Pope Alexander VI read similarly. He fathered several children whom he later maneuvered into positions of power, overtly bribed his way into the papacy, raised money by assassinating land owners and then seizing their property, and died of poison that he had probably prepared for a guest, but then mistakenly took himself (Kelly, p. 54). With such behavior in mind, Barnes was willing to assert that "to no succession of men who have ever lived could the appellative, *'the* man of sin,[1] be applied with so much propriety as to this succession" (Albert Barnes, *Notes on the New Testament* [Grand Rapids, Mich.: Baker Book House, 1955], vol. 8, p. 82).

To some interpreters it is simply not sufficient to say that Paul's words can apply to Rome at one point in time, to the papacy at another point in time, and to Satan as the power behind it all at still another point in time. But no single entity seems to quite measure up to all the terms Paul used. Furthermore, no single individual fits all the categories either. It seems the best we can do is to set forth the theory with the least objections and let the reader decide. That theory, in the author's opinion, is that Paul, with prophetic vision, could see the enemy working against the church of

Christ with increasing vigor, but held under some restraint for the time being, probably by God. But the time will come when that restraint is removed, and even greater hostility and difficulties will follow, until the advent finally puts an end to the controversy once and for all. If modern interpreters can put a name and a face to an adversary that Paul described only with metaphors, they should do so with caution and with tolerance for those who hold other views.

The only other real "issue" in this short letter is the idleness of believers, which had grown worse since the first letter. Their preoccupation with the imminence of the advent had resulted in a posture of "sit and wait," for the Lord was about to deliver them. With vigor, Paul reminded them how he worked to sustain himself and how he now expected the same of them. In fact, there is a certain bite to his counsel: "If any one will not work, let him not eat" (3:10). Such wisdom is always appropriate. It is imperative for believers to work while they wait and "in quietness . . . earn their own living" (3:12). And if the wait seems longer than expected, the admonition is simple: "Do not be weary in well-doing" (3:13).

Additional readings on chapter 3
1. Acts 17:1-9.
2. Ellen G. White, *The Acts of the Apostles*, pp. 221-230; 255-268.
3. Leon Morris, *The First and Second Epistles to the Thessalonians*, vol. 20 of *The New International Commentary on the New Testament*, ed. F. F. Bruce (Grand Rapids, Mich.: Eerdmans, 1973).

Chapter
Four

A Divided City—
a Divided Church

Introduction to 1 Corinthians

A two-party system may be good for politics, but it wreaks havoc in a small church, and a four-party system is sheer disaster. In first-century Corinth, the infant Christian church seemed about to self-destruct (1:11, 12). Small groups within the church had become so attached to a favorite preacher that noisy arguments replaced meaningful worship. Given the Corinthian environment, however, such factiousness should come as no great surprise. The great seaport city, capital of the Roman province of Achaia, caught up in commercial enterprises and sensual pursuits, was not the setting for a carefully reasoned philosophy of life or for a calm, orderly religion. On the one hand were merchants whose wealth had accrued from their financial shrewdness, and on the other hand were toilers who lived and worked for the next meal. Since the main business of Corinth involved transportation of people and goods, there was little time for genuine science and art. Unscrupulous merchants, disciplined athletes, and pleasure-loving crowds were all convinced that every person could pursue whatever seemed right in his own eyes.

> Corinth had amusements in plenty, wholesome and
> otherwise, a theatre seating 18,000 . . . [a] music hall
> with 3,000 seats, the Isthmian athletic games, itiner-
> ant musicians, dancers . . . and, of course, the
> thousand prostitutes of Aphrodite (Sherman E. John-
> son, *Paul the Apostle and His Cities* [Wilmington, Del.:
> Michael Glazier, 1987], p. 98).

Moral corruption had become so identified with the city
that the Greeks coined the verb to "Corinthianize," which
meant "to act immorally."

Understandably, the same frenzy that characterized the
social and secular pursuits left its stamp on the religious
practices of Corinth. In the various temples throughout the
city, Aphrodite, the goddess of love, was venerated by practices that were little better than legalized prostitution. All this
had a bearing on how the first Christians of the area perceived
and practiced their Christianity. It was also reflected in some
of the counsel they later received from Paul, their spiritual
father.

The apostle

It was with flagging enthusiasm and considerable fear
about the future that Paul first entered the city of Corinth.
He was alone, having sent Timothy back to Macedonia for
a progress report (1 Thess. 3:1), and he was still smarting
from the mocking treatment handed him by the Athenian
philosophers (Acts 17:32, 33). A short time earlier, the
Philippians had beaten, imprisoned, and expelled him from
their town, following which, to save his life, he was forced
to flee from both Thessalonica and Berea. Then the
Athenian philosophers humiliated him. With all of that in
his recent past, he had a right to feel discouraged. It
certainly should come as no surprise that, when he lets us
in on his feelings of that time, he admits to "much fear and
trembling" (1 Cor. 2:3). Little wonder, then, that the Lord
came to him with a message of courage and comfort ("Do not
be afraid . . . I am with you," Acts 18:9, 10). Buoyed up with
such divine encouragement, he found the stamina to buck

the opposition in that city for a year and a half (Acts 18:11), a rather lengthy stay for Paul.

The Corinthian correspondence

In addition to 1 and 2 Corinthians, we know of at least two other letters that passed between Paul and the Corinthians, and possibly a third. In 1 Corinthians 5:9, Paul alludes to a former letter in which he had instructed the believers "not to associate with immoral men." Except for this brief reference, this precanonical letter is a complete mystery. In addition, Paul makes reference to a letter the Corinthians had sent to him. In 1 Corinthians 7:1 he said, "Now concerning the matters about which you wrote." While the details of their inquiries are not clear, there is reason to believe that the issues discussed in chapters 8, 12, and 16 were included in the letter the Corinthians sent to Paul. A possible fifth letter may be referred to in 2 Corinthians 2:4 as the "painful letter," which Paul says he composed in "much affliction and anguish . . . with many tears." Since that description does not fit most of 1 Corinthians, some scholars have suggested that the strident, reproving tone of 2 Corinthians 10 through 13 may have actually comprised that "painful letter," and thus that section originally preceded chapters 1 through 9. Yet the message in chapters 10 through 13 is not all painfully reproving. In fact, in 11:11 and 12:14, 15, 19, Paul reminds the believers that his great concern arises only out of his deep love for them. The fact is, references to the "painful letter" are simply too cryptic to identify it with certainty. Its separate existence and content remain only a hazy impression.

The Corinthian visits

A certain mystery also marks Paul's visits to Corinth. There is little question about his first visit, which planted the church (Acts 18:1-11), or his final visit on his third journey (Acts 20:2). However, 2 Corinthians 12:14 and 13:1 refer to this final visit as the third one, yet no details are given about any second visit to Corinth. The hypothesis is that after Paul wrote some of his reproving concerns in 1 Corinthians (see 5:9) or gave the counsel in the mysterious "painful letter," he was so anguished about how the Corinthians received the admonition that he made a quick trip to Corinth to determine for himself their reaction. This hasty visit may have been somewhat unsuccessful; hence, he could say in 2 Corinthians 2:1 that he didn't want to have another painful visit with them. According to this hypothesis, Paul's visit to Corinth on his third journey, which followed his writing of 2 Corinthians, would indeed be his third visit.

Historical setting

At the time Paul wrote 1 Corinthians, he was living in Ephesus, having stopped there early on his third missionary journey. He remained in Ephesus three years, his longest recorded stay in any city. While there, his intense curiosity about the progress of the church in Corinth was somewhat satisfied by the reports brought by Apollos (16:12), a group mentioned in 16:17, and members of the household of Chloe (1:11). He seemed to be writing the letter near the end of his three-year stay in Ephesus, as he was planning to visit Corinth soon (16:6-8), where he hoped to stay through the winter until Pentecost. Accordingly, it seems reasonable to date the letter either late in A.D. 56 or early 57.

Occasion of the epistle

News that Paul received from the various messengers from Corinth gave rise to the epistle. Some of the news was reason for rejoicing, but most was cause for concern. Since the causes for concern were numerous, it is difficult to identify just one theme in the letter. In fact, in none of Paul's epistles is there such a variety of problems addressed as in 1 Corinthians. The issues here run the gamut from the relatively simple problem of personal offerings to the evil of condoned incest. Thus, Paul hoped to achieve several goals by his letter. First, he sought to unify a fragmented group. A divisive spirit of hero worship had split the church into factions, giving rise to Paul's call for unity. Next, he attacked the permissiveness that had become so pervasive that gross immorality was being tolerated (5:1). Finally, he gave instruction on a variety of questions that had perplexed the members.

If one main theme runs through the letter, it might be called "the meaning of freedom." The Corinthian Christians flaunted the idea that Christ brings freedom, to the extent that they tolerated almost any behavior (5:1, 2, 6). In reaction, Paul said that the life of the believer must be ruled by love and a sense of responsibility for the growth of the entire membership (13; 14:26). Put simply, the theme of 1 Corinthians is an extended explanation of the nature of Christian freedom. The epistle nowhere defines the concept in so many words. It simply shows how Christian freedom should respond to numerous problem situations, and the believer or the church is left to make the necessary additional applications.

Additional readings on chapter 4

1. Gordon D. Fee, *The First Epistle to the Corinthians, The New International Commentary on the New Testament*, ed. F. F. Bruce (Grand Rapids, Mich.: Eerdmans, 1987).

2. Roy Harrisville, *Augsburg Commentary on the New Testament: 1 Corinthians* (Minneapolis, Minn.: Augsburg, 1987).

3. James Moffatt, *The First Epistle of Paul to the Corinthians, The Moffatt New Testament Commentary* (London: Hodder and Stoughton, 1939).

4. Ellen G. White, *The Acts of the Apostles*, pp. 243-254; 269-280.

5. Review Acts 18:1-18 for the events that took place while Paul was in Corinth the first time.

Chapter

Five

Corinthian Christians— a Progress Report?

1 Corinthians 1-6

Chapter 1—How to be saints without being saintly

When is Christian living all it should be? Is it possible for a person or a church to reach a level of totally spotless living? Here's an easier question: Is it conceivable that a Christian or a group of Christians might live *below* their potential? To this last question, Paul would have shouted, "Yes, and they live in Corinth!"

However, before he addresses their flaws and foibles, he surprises us by calling them "saints" who have been "sanctified" (1:2). So which is it going to be, saints or sinners? Beginning in chapter 1:11 and continuing in virtually every chapter, Paul's reproofs are specific and sometimes biting. How is it that saints can be so unsaintly? It appears that his use of the term is at least paradoxical if not satirical.

In actual fact, it may be neither. While the Greek term can be translated "holy ones," it is clear in numerous passages like this one that Paul used the term, not as a precise description of character, but rather as a tender term of identity, akin to the more contemporary "fellow believers" or the overworked "brothers and sisters." Of course, if the term served the additional purpose of gently prodding them toward the goal of holiness, so much the better. But it appears that to be a member of the community of believers was, for Paul, to be one of the saints—which says little about their saintliness. Thus Paul could call them saints and then rebuke them unsparingly for unsaintly activities, since the term was primarily meant to indicate that they were members of the family of God. Paul was like a father who would stop at nothing to defend his own family from an outside attack, yet have no qualms about meting out his own brand of correctives for his children. Consequently, there is no real paradox between the terms of endearment in 1:2-8 and later stern reproofs.

For a communicator, it is a draining, discouraging experience to be frequently reminded that your message is not only unacceptable, but is worthy only of ridicule and scorn. Paul, the seemingly untiring evangelist, sometimes grew weary of the verbal jousting, and that fatigue is noticeable in chapters 1:8–2:5. He must have had the words *folly* (1:18, 21, 23) or *foolish[ness]* (20, 25, 27) thrown his direction several times, as often as he repeated them.

In this setting, he recounted in chapter 2:1-4 his early days in Corinth, when his spirit was less than exuberant. He had come to them directly from a less than spectacular response in Athens (Acts 17:32, 33), with no traveling companions (18:5), and needing encouragement (18:9). Remembering those days, he reminded the Corinthians that a power outside of himself enabled him to overcome his weakness and fear (2:3). In fact, having had a little time to reflect, he was more than ever committed to proclaiming that the very issue which the Greeks called folly and which the Jews stumbled over, the crucified Christ (2:2), is the essence of spiritual life (1:30).

Chapter 2—Only God's Spirit can unlock spiritual puzzles

In 2:6-16 Paul set forth an important truth about spiritual perception. He explained how some people could appear so blind to something that was obvious to others. He attributed the phenomenon to something he called spiritual discernment, and he illustrated the point by contrasting natural, physiological abilities such as seeing and hearing with the ability to understand spiritual concepts. In that setting, his quote from Isaiah in verse 9 shows that what the physical eyes and ears cannot make known to us, God's Spirit can and already has. Accordingly, the familiar interpretation that relegates the unperceived thing of verse 9 to the beauties of heavenly mansions is too limiting. Paul explicitly states in verse 10 that whatever it is in verse 9 which the natural eye and ear cannot perceive, it has been made clear to us by the Holy Spirit. Obviously, the unfathomed scenes of heaven are outside of Paul's concern here. Rather, he contrasts the perceptions of "rulers of this age" (2:8) with those of people who have been enlightened by the Spirit of God. The real meaning of the crucified Christ, which Paul calls the "hidden wisdom of God" (2:7), can only be grasped by a spiritual "seeing" and "hearing." It is simply not available to the physical senses. While the same can be said about heavenly realities, these do not seem to have been in Paul's mind in this context. The *SDA Bible Commentary* makes a twofold application of the passage by distinguishing between a *primary* application (present spiritual realities) and an application by *extension* (the beauties of heaven).

Chapter 3—The folly of hero worship

Having established that humans have a "spiritual" dimension, Paul, in chapter 3, related that notion to his earlier assertion that the Corinthians were not exactly living up to their potential. He spelled it out by the analogy of eating and stated that at this point in their spiritual growth they should have been able to take solid food, but instead they were still slurping the fare of spiritual babies. He implied that there is a time and place for living as babies and being fed with milk, but for them, that time had passed. His metaphor continues as he contrasts milk with meat or solid food. His figure of milk probably represented the missionary preaching he had done at first, while the solid food referred to the more advanced preaching to growing Christians, who should by now have been ready to move beyond the rudiments of the Christian faith to more complex issues.

The evidence he offered of their spiritual stagnation was a divisive brand of hero worship, which he first underscored in chapter 1. A party spirit creates not only problems occasioned by jealousy and factional struggles, which hinder positive advances, but is also the danger that human heroes will displace God Himself. Paul explicitly warned of such when he showed in verse 5 that the human agents are only tools of God, who alone can bring the necessary growth. He stressed the same thing in verse 9, where he introduced three more analogies ("God's fellow workers," "God's field," "God's building"), and in each case, the word emphasized is *God.* Thus, Paul repeatedly directed attention away from the human agent to the really important influence, which is God.

It is interesting to note that when chapter 3:3, 4 is read alongside 1:7, we get the picture of a very religion-oriented community, very involved and enthusiastic about their religious leaders, yet harboring petty jealousies that were actually quite irreligious. In fact, Paul reminded them that when they tried to live the new life by the old party spirit, they were simply being carnal in a new way. Religious profession can never make a loveless life a spiritual life. Furthermore, it seems clear from 3:4, 5 that neither Paul nor Apollos had intentionally curried the favor of the people. They had simply done their work as messengers of the gospel, but the people found it easier to become attached to individuals than to seek a deepening experience with God.

In his analogies in chapter 3:9, Paul described his past missionary activities in agricultural language—he had planted, Apollos had watered, and God had caused the growth. This figure stresses the passive nature of the believer—a field is merely a recipient of the tilling and planting process. But then Paul turned to another figure that stresses a more active role for the Christian—you are God's building. As Paul worked out his meaning, it becomes clear that his real emphasis was on the act of building.

Paul's illustrations often twisted and turned as he explained himself, and such is the case here. The foundation of the building seems clear enough. After all, what is unclear about stating that Christ is our real foundation? But after that, things get a little fuzzy. In chapter 3:12 Paul refers to building on the foundation with "gold, silver, precious stones, wood, hay, straw"—truly strange materials for any conceivable building project! Of the six things mentioned, only wood is a reasonable building material. In this extended and complicated figure of speech, Paul appears to introduce two contrasting ideas—*value* and *flammability*. Gold, silver, and precious stones would make odd building materials, but they do represent things of great value.

In contrast, wood is an acceptable building material, but hay and stubble seem more related to the next figure in verse 13, which is fire. In that connection, wood, hay, and stubble are all of little value because of their flammability. So, by means of these contrasting figures, Paul illustrated his point: The work of building, whether of character or of buildings, must be done with materials that are both valuable and lasting.

However, analyzing Paul's figures too carefully can be a confusing endeavor, since it is not the facts but the overall meaning of the facts that Paul hopes to make clear. Just so, in this passage, while the meaning of each figure may still be debated, the overall intent seems quite clear: Careless teaching, like careless building, may result in tragic loss of the work in a very short time.

Verse 15 has also caused some perplexity, since it seems to suggest a narrow escape for some whose work is destroyed. It helps to keep in mind that Paul was directing his admonitions primarily to teacher/builders like himself (see 10, 12, 14). Consequently, when he referred in verse 15 to a man's work, he was not talking about a person's individual spiritual activities, but to a minister's work—that is, his students or converts. Accordingly, he was at the same time urging careful building and offering encouragement to those who had built poorly. Apparently, for some teachers, it was too late to urge that they teach with care—they had already taught poorly, even erroneously. Yet Paul did not devastate them, but offered a glimmer of hope—their work (i.e., some converts) might be lost, but genuine confession could save the teachers, even though the loss of those they misled would be extremely painful.

Just how important Paul viewed the issue of Christian influence is seen in his next figure in verses 16, 17. In God's sight, the collective community of believers is His temple, in which His Spirit dwells. Anyone who fragments or in any way threatens the stability and vital life of this living temple brings upon himself a most serious threat from God. Whoever touches God's corporate body, the church, touches the apple of His eye. Some have made an application of verses 16, 17 to caring for our body-temples, but that interpretation fits 6:19, 20 rather than 3:16, 17. Here, the context clearly refers to the collective body of Christ, which is His church.

Paul concluded chapter 3 on the same note with which he began the chapter—the foolishness of fragmented human loyalties. He stressed that it is not only wrong, but foolish for anyone to give undue deference to any human agent, when all the good of all the human agents is summed up in Christ, and He is accessible to all. How foolish to settle for the good qualities of a lowly Peter or Paul when you can have it all in the Christ of God!

Chapter 4—Pride makes servants think they are kings

Apparently the leaders in the Corinthian church looked upon themselves in pretty glowing colors. In contrast, Paul felt that servanthood implied a more lowly assessment. The Corinthian practice of setting up human heroes or ministers and making petty choices between them, passing judgment on them, approving some and disapproving others, Paul ridiculed in verses 3-5 as not only unwise but invalid. Since his (Paul's) judging abilities were flawed, chances are theirs were too. Consequently, it was better to allow God to do all the judging. In the process, rivalry would be put aside, pride would be dethroned, and they would be commended by God (5). But apparently their feelings of pride were firmly entrenched, for Paul seized on some rather forceful satire to bring them down to size. His sarcastic irony in verse 8 artificially exalted them ("you have become kings"), yet it was actually designed to humble them, especially in view of the stark contrast he drew between their supposed heights and the apostles' depths described in verses 9, 10 ("we are fools for Christ's sake"). The catalog of suffering that followed (10-13) was not given to draw sympathy so much as to humble those arrogant ones who had become puffed up, an attitude that sucked out the lifeblood of the Corinthian church.

Chapter 5—When tolerance becomes arrogance

Chapter 5 focuses on one particular case of immorality that surpasses all others. But two things upset Paul—the incest, and the arrogance that could excuse such behavior. To Paul, it was appalling enough that a man was living with his stepmother, but it was also troubling that the Corinthians not only tolerated, but apparently condoned such behavior (2, 6). The Mediterranean people had a way of looking upon religion as something apart from moral behavior. In fact, it was not uncommon for immoral practices to actually be a part of their religious rituals. The close connection they made between fertility rites and religion brought together some otherwise very incompatible activities. In their attempt to be open-minded and tolerant, some members in the Corinthian church had, with a good deal of pride, espoused the liberal view that now "all things are lawful" (6:12; 10:23). Apparently, misunderstanding the meaning of "freedom in Christ" had led some members to confuse that freedom with license, and thereby actually boast that their church allowed members complete freedom to be themselves. But Paul would have none of it. Both the man in question and the arrogant boasting were to be put away.

At the same time Paul made clear that such disassociation was not intended to cut off fellowship with unbelievers, for that would severely curtail evangelism. Rather, he wanted no accord between believers and those who would bring the world and its ways into the church, thereby destroying the gospel message. In limiting his counsel to this one particular case of immorality and arrogance, Paul provided no instruction manual on methods of church discipline. Any attempt to extrapolate from this chapter procedures for disciplining other types of infractions should probably be avoided.

Chapter 6—Is it selfish to get what you deserve?

Paul's opinion of Roman magistrates was generally favorable, but the language in chapter 6 seems to suggest otherwise. However, in spite of his reference to the unrighteous (1), the real issue is not the moral rectitude of the judges but the behavior of the Christians in the presence of nonbelievers. Paul was always very sensitive to the missionary witness the church gave, and it was clear to him that to have non-Christian judges adjudicating petty squabbles between Christians would bring only disrepute upon the cause of Christ. Obviously, Corinth had no Christian judges at this time. Hence, Paul asked the members to handle their own "trivial cases." His reasoning reflects the great distance he believed existed between the realm of the saints and that of the unrighteous. Accordingly, he reminded the believers that the time would come when they would sit in judgment over the world and over angels, so surely they were competent to solve the arguments that then troubled them. He seems to say, Since the unrighteous will one day sit at your bar of justice, how foolish that you now place yourselves at theirs.

Nevertheless, the passage does not preclude all legal action for all Christians for all time. It is reasonable to conclude that when the case is not trivial, and when all judges are not unrighteous, the reputation of the church might not necessarily be degraded by any and all legal action. "To deduce from vs. 1 that any going to court is forbidden to Christians is unwarranted. In a Christian country jurisprudence is a blessing from God if it reckons with the laws given by the Lord" (F. W. Grosheide, *Commentary on the First Epistle to the Corinthians, The New International Commentary on the New Testament*, ed. F. F. Bruce [Grand Rapids, Mich.: Eerdmans, 1974], p. 133). Of course, such action is unfortunate, but in a world of sin and ruthless sinners, legal action may, on rare occasions, be the only way some injustices can be corrected. Viewed through the eyes of Paul, the foremost question is one's Christian witness, which, he felt, most litigation damaged. Accordingly, it is preferable for the individual to suffer loss than to demand his or her rights, if, in the process of gaining his or her rights, the cause of Christ should be shamed.

In verses 9-11 Paul again emphasized the distance that exists between the righteous and the unrighteous, the members and nonmembers. He did not say the Corinthians were guilty of all these evils but simply enumerated some characteristic sins of the pagans and hinted that the recent behavior of certain Christians was getting dangerously close to behavior of the unrighteous. But verse 11 is a reminder of the dramatic difference between believers and unbelievers, between what they *were* and what they *are*. The implication is that they should act like what they are—baptized members of the household of faith.

The meaning and implications of "Christian freedom" often cause extended discussion, and 1 Corinthians 6:12-20 indicates that the Corinthians had not solved the puzzle. Apparently they thought they had solved it, for they were widely trumpeting their newfound freedom. The phrase "All things are lawful for me" is given twice in 6:12 and twice in 10:23 in such a way as to suggest that Paul here quoted an oft-heard line of the Corinthians. But it was clear to Paul that Corinthian "freedom" had turned into license to behave however the people pleased. In this context, Paul addressed only the problem of immorality, since that had been such a prevalent part of their lives as pagans and was apparently still being tolerated, in spite of their recent conversion to Christianity.

Additional readings on chapter 5

1. Gordon D. Fee, *The First Epistle to the Corinthians, The New International Commentary on the New Testament*, ed. F. F. Bruce (Grand Rapids, Mich.: Eerdmans, 1987).
2. Roy Harrisville, *Augsburg Commentary on the New Testament: 1 Corinthians* (Minneapolis, Minn.: Augsburg, 1987).
3. James Moffatt, *The First Epistle of Paul to the Corinthians, The Moffatt New Testament Commentary* (London: Hodder and Stoughton, 1939).
4. Ellen G. White, *The Acts of the Apostles*, pp. 298-308.
5. Review Acts 18:1-18 for the events that took place while Paul was in Corinth the first time.

Chapter
Six

Paul Responds to Corinthian Questions

1 Corinthians 7-11

Chapter 7—Questions about marriage

Although the Corinthian Christians were a scrappy bunch, many were making serious efforts to understand their newfound faith. When questions about Christian living arose, they turned to their first teacher for straight answers, and this brings us to chapter 7. Here Paul addressed the first of several questions that plagued these novice Christians. It would be helpful if we had a copy of their inquiries. Instead, we have only Paul's answers, which means that we must infer their questions from his answers, and this is not exactly a precise endeavor. Still, the major concerns are rather clear. Obviously, the Corinthians were wondering about the impact of Christianity upon various aspects of marriage. In general, Paul seems torn between a sympathy for celibacy on the one hand and a desire to reprove those extremists who totally disparaged marriage on the other. In Corinth, the extremes met.

58

Paul began by stating his approval of the single state. Most scholars agree that the statement in verse 1 about a man "touching" a woman is a euphemism for sex, which, in Paul's view, implied marriage. His comment may have been a response to both Jewish and Roman attitudes of the time. Jewish men were expected to marry, often at a young age, and Roman laws had recently been passed that encouraged marriage and discouraged celibacy. With that in mind, some in Corinth may have wondered if Christians were allowed to remain unmarried. Paul answered with a vigorous Yes, but quickly added some qualifiers.

No sooner did he reassure the unmarried ones that they should consider themselves normal even though single than he hastened to add a pragmatic observation: "But remember, temptation is at hand, so better to be married and safe, than almost celibate and sorry." Such reasoning sounds like Paul viewed marriage as simply an escape from guilt or wrong-doing, which is hardly an exalted view of the married state. But such a conclusion needs more evidence than this passage. In any case, pragmatism is a frequent thread in the fabric of Paul's counsels.

Having approved the celibate state in verse 1 and the appropriateness of marriage in verse 2, Paul proceeded in verses 3-5 to counsel the married members that they should not attempt to practice continence within marriage. Apparently some married people in Corinth were remaining celibate, and Paul warned that the dangers of such behavior outweighed any possible good. A married couple should proceed with such a plan only by mutual consent for a limited time and with a spiritual purpose. Even then, the pressures and temptations are great—Satan will be close at hand to tempt "through lack of self-control" (5). Only the principle of love and concern for one another should govern the sexual expression of husband and wife. Also, in view of his comments elsewhere that seem to disparage the status of women, it is interesting to note Paul's stress on the equality of the partners in this matter of sexual needs and expression. In that time it must have come as quite a shock to hear that "the husband does not rule over his own body, but the wife does" (4). Paul's supposed chauvinism has gotten much more press than it deserves!

In verse 6, Paul explains that what he has just said is not in the form of a law, but is rather his informed opinion. Some have used this comment, along with his disclaimer in verse 12 ("I say, not the Lord"), as the basis for ignoring whatever in the chapter seems difficult or out of keeping with societal expectations. His opinion, under these circumstances, supposedly carries no more weight than the opinion of any other Christian leader. However, his similar comment in verse 25 is quite helpful. There he notes, "I have no command of the Lord, but I give my opinion as one who by the Lord's mercy is trustworthy." His point seems to be that while on certain questions he has not had an explicit revelation from the Lord, he feels his opinion on the subject should carry weight, since it is, by God's mercy, a trustworthy opinion. Furthermore, while every idea Paul had was not infallible, those thoughts expressed in Scripture dare not be looked upon as merely human ideas that are no better than yours or mine. When his ideas are given in the form of admonition and carry the weight of inspiration, they must be taken very seriously and considered as part of the overall Word, which has been preserved through the centuries for our learning.

In verses 7-9 Paul expressed his clear preference for the single state but acknowledged that to successfully carry it out, one must have help from the Lord, which he called a "gift"—and not all have that gift. So, contrary to the popular ideas of his time, Paul asserted that the single state is an acceptable alternative to the married state—but only for those who have the gift of control over their desires for sexual expression. As mentioned before, such an interpretation seems to represent a rather utilitarian view of marriage, but it also makes clear that sexual expression is only to take place within the bounds of marriage. Thus, Paul seems to be saying that just as the sex drive is a God-given part of our being, so marriage is the God-given state wherein that expression is to take place.

In verses 10, 11, Paul reminded the Corinthians of the teaching of Jesus ("Not I, but the Lord") regarding divorce, thus indicating that nothing had changed since Jesus made clear that Christian marriage is not to be broken (Mark 10:11, 12). Paul did not here deal with any of the endless "exceptional circumstances" that seem to be the preoccupation of modern-day Christians. He simply reiterated the rule Jesus set forth: Marriage is for life.

Paul turned in verses 12-16 to the question of mixed marriages—a new problem in the church. Jesus had not addressed such a situation because a split marriage—one Christian, one unbeliever—could not exist until the Christian community had developed enough cohesiveness to polarize marriage partners. When that should happen, Paul made it plain that any split in the marriage is be initiated only by the unbelieving partner. At that point, the Christian is to follow the path of peace and not oppose the departure of the unbelieving spouse. Of course, it is assumed that the believing partner has given no provocation except the adoption of the Christian faith. If such a split takes place, and the unbeliever leaves for good, "the brother or sister is not bound" (15). Does that phrase mean that the innocent Christian divorced person is free to remarry? Probably, yes.

The strange-sounding figure in verse 14 of the Christian spouse consecrating the unbeliever may have arisen from the fear of some members that marriage to an unbeliever would impart some ritual impurity to the believer. Paul offered the reassurance that not only is there no such transfer of "pollution," but rather a transfer of "holiness." Still, he did not suggest that marriage would automatically convert the unbeliever. He seems to be saying that marriage incorporates a principle of family solidarity whereby if only "one of the pair possesses the divine 'holiness,' that is sufficient to 'consecrate' the other and to render the children also 'sacred' to God, instead of leaving them outside the pale" (James Moffatt, *The First Epistle of Paul to the Corinthians, The Moffatt New Testament Commentary* [London: Hodder and Stoughton, 1939], p. 82). Accordingly, Paul here used the terms *consecrate* or *sanctify* in more of a liturgical or ritual sense than in an ethical sense.

The dynamic, outspoken Paul hardly seems the type to opt for the status quo. Yet in verses 17-24, that seems to be what he is doing. Although slaves were allowed to seek their freedom, Paul here suggested that they not try to change the social condition of things. So, in whatever state each was when converted to Christianity, in that state he should remain (24). This passage can be understood only in the light of Paul's conviction that a time of distress was imminent. Paul clearly felt that the present state of things was about to pass away, so the usual concerns for social change must be put aside. In Paul's mind was only one question: "How must we live in the face of the coming cataclysm?"

Understanding this preoccupation of Paul is essential to a proper understanding of not only verses 17-24, but also Paul's following comments on marriage. Thus, the main idea in verses 25-35 is the importance of having single-minded devotion to the Lord because the "time has grown very short" (29). All important decisions (such as taking a spouse) were to be made in light of the shortness of time. In fact, if one idea is the key to understanding all of 1 Corinthians 7, it is that "the time of distress is at hand."

A closely related question is brought up in verses 36-38. Some interpreters have looked upon these verses as counsel to a father as to whether he should allow his virgin daughter to marry. However, the reference to "his passions" in verse 36 and the contrast in verses 37 and 38 between keeping his betrothed or marrying her favor the view that Paul here counseled a young man who was debating whether to marry his fiancée. As mentioned above, while some Corinthian Christians felt every male should be married, certain ascetics apparently felt that celibacy was the only acceptable practice for Christians. Here Paul addressed the latter notion and repeated to the engaged couple the same counsel he had given to the unmarried in verses 8, 9—the single state is preferable ("in view of the impending distress," verse 26), but marriage is fitting and proper. The engaged couple obviously had strong feelings for one another (the translation "pass the flower of her age" in the KJV is not supported by the Greek), and Paul assured them that those feelings did not have to be forever denied, since marriage is perfectly acceptable for Christians.

Chapter 8—On eating sacrificial meat and being a good role model

One of the most painful realities of growing up is the gradual awareness that our actions and words must be related. Everyone knows that parenthood involves a heavy dose of modeling to support the teaching, but long before we become parents, someone reminds us that "little brother is looking up to us," and we groan at the thought of having to live consistently. Because the example in 1 Corinthians 8 is so foreign to us (meat sacrificed to idols?), the simple but powerful admonitions about Christian responsibility sail right over our heads. The first issue raised was not simply the appropriateness of idol worship. That question had already been put to rest by the Jerusalem Council (Acts 15:20, 29). Still, just in case any lingering questions remained about that, Paul belittled the validity of idols by ridiculing their very existence (4). But Corinthians still had uncertainties about a few related practices. Those who, like Paul, believed idols to be nothing realized that food dedicated to "nothing" was no different from any other food. But some in the church could not so easily brush off all the ritual impurity that clung to idols and their worshipers. For such members to eat food that had been previously offered to idols would require a compromise, or a "defiling" of their consciences. So Paul addressed two distinct groups in chapter 8: those who were of strong conscience, for whom an idol and its offering meant nothing; and those of weak conscience, who still believed that an idol and the food offered to it could cause pollution.

In verses 1-3 Paul addressed those of strong conscience, who were smugly content with their "knowledge" about such things and were not exactly concerned for those babes in the faith who still thought that idols could actually cause some kind of ritual defilement. Accordingly, Paul drew the unusual contrast between knowledge and love. He asserted that one's knowledge (in verse 9, he used the term *liberty*) must be controlled by love, or the person would simply be puffed up. But when love controls the way a person uses his knowledge, the result is a building up.

Clearly, Paul's concern in the chapter has nothing to do with diet, as such, and everything to do with the impact of one's influence on others. Because some translations have rendered the phrase, "meat sacrificed to idols," some have seen a connection here to vegetarianism. While it is true that flesh meat was probably the most common form of food offered to idols, the word *broma*, used throughout this chapter, means simply food. Furthermore, Paul's comment in verse 8 that "food will not commend us to God" clearly refers to a broad principle relating to a personal attitude, not to a specific article of diet.

In verses 4-6 he commented on the foolishness of believing in gods, thus instructing the members who were of weak conscience. While Paul was very concerned about his influence on the weaker brethren, he was also concerned to educate their weak consciences and make them stronger.

Having attempted briefly to educate the weaker brother about idols in verses 7-13, Paul addressed his most explicit remarks to the strong members, who did not let love control their behavior toward their weaker brothers. Paul here shows just how important our influence is on another: "If my example can lead another to sin against his conscience, I will never again eat sacrificial meat."

The conscientious Christian is indeed his brother's keeper.

Chapter 9—On giving up rights for a noble cause

As an apostle of strong conscience, Paul knew that certain behaviors were inappropriate for Christians. But he also knew that other forms of behavior were so "appropriate" that he called them a "right." In chapter 9 he gave various examples of these rights, such as the right to food and drink and the right to be "accompanied by a wife." To illustrate his point he referred to soldiers who were paid for their service, farmers who were fed by their own vineyards, shepherds who were fed from their own flocks, and, finally, the lowly oxen that help themselves to the grain they thresh. Each example was meant to underscore the "rights" to certain privileges. But the main "right," in Paul's mind, was the right to receive financial support from the members. However, after thoroughly establishing his point about his rights, he proceeded in verse 12 to make his primary point—he had renounced his rights. His reasoning was closely tied to that of the previous chapter. He did not want to set an example that could even appear greedy. Therefore, even though he deserved to be paid for his services, he would earn his own way so no one could accuse him of preaching simply for profit (12, 15).

Single-mindedness is not narrow-mindedness, and Paul was single-minded. In fact, he clearly revealed the intensity of his focus in verses 19-23, where he summarized the controlling preoccupation of his life and ministry—"I have become all things to all men, that I might by all means save some." It is possible to abuse his principle by turning it into simple utilitarian reasoning, where the end justifies the means. However, it would be unfair to Paul to apply this rule to other areas of decision making, when he specifically relates it only to his soul-winning activities. He simply wanted to make clear to the world his priority of values, with the hope that somehow his example in this matter would become the norm for all.

Self-discipline is never thought of as entertaining, but Paul gave new meaning to the phrase, "no pain, no gain." "I pommel my body and subdue it," he stated (27). Such rigor could be misunderstood, as if he, like the ascetics, considered his body inherently evil and therefore fit only for punishment. But Paul elsewhere made it clear that the real enemy to be overcome is sin (Rom. 6:12, 14), and sin is only incidentally related to the physical body. Clearly the language in verse 27 is figurative and is used to illustrate the forcefulness one needs to be a single-minded, victorious Christian. Accordingly, Paul here made a statement against the "cheap grace" concept that once a commitment to Christ has been made, any further commitment is not only foolish, but theologically wrong. But if Paul felt that constant discipline of will was necessary, "lest after preaching to others I myself should be disqualified," then surely other Christians must be similarly disciplined. Apparently, through careless neglect, even spiritual stalwarts may lose all in the end. The familiar idea "once saved, always saved" did not originate with Paul.

Chapter 10—The tragic example of Israel

Having just given the "strong" believers a warning against carelessness, Paul then turned to the most tragic example he could think of—the experience of Israel. His meaning is quite clear, for after listing their various sins—idolatry, fornication, presumption, and unbelief (7-10)—he brought his argument to a head in verses 11, 12: "These things happened to them as a warning, but they were written down for our instruction. . . . Therefore let any one who thinks that he stands take heed." Clearly, Paul was talking to those believers who considered themselves of strong conscience. No one should think of himself as too strong to fail. But Paul hastened to add in verse 13 that God faithfully monitors our trials, and we can rest in the assurance that He will not allow us to be overwhelmed.

In verses 23-30 Paul referred again to the slogan that some Corinthians apparently used to flaunt their Christian liberty: "All things are lawful." As in chapter 6, he qualified that liberty with two limitations. The first is the same as in chapter 6: "Not all things are helpful"; but the second is different: "Not all things build up." Here, my indiscriminate practice of "all things" affects the other person, and that other person is once again the less mature, or weak-conscience, believer. This is the same point that Paul treated in chapter 8, only here he added a few more details. Portions of animals sacrificed for idol worship were often sold in the marketplace. Since this meat could not be differentiated from other meat, a Christian might inadvertently purchase meat that had been sacrificed to an idol. In chapter 8, most of Paul's comments were meant to encourage the strong brethren to treat with compassion the scruples of the weak. But in chapter 10:25-27, he added the thought that the strong brother could go ahead and eat the food (broma), as long as he had no reason to believe that exercising his liberty would lead the weaker Christian astray. After all, there was nothing inherently defiling in the food sold in the marketplace, nor in that same food if it was served on a neighbor's table.

Verses 28, 29 appear to be a sudden reversal of thought, based on deference to the weaker brother ("out of consideration for . . . his conscience . . . do not eat it"). The RSV suggests such an interpretation by setting off these verses in parentheses. So here, as in chapter 8, Paul recommended that concern for the conscience of the weaker brother might cause the stronger brother to defer and not eat. Then suddenly, in the last half of verse 29, Paul picked up the thread he dropped at the end of verse 27 and added that in some circumstances, one's freedom of action need not be controlled by another person's scruples. Thus in verse 29 Paul repeated the idea of verses 25, 26 in a slightly different form and once again defended the freedom of a dinner guest in a pagan home to eat whatever sacrificial meat his host set before him. Paul attempted the delicate balancing act of teaching the mature Christian to use his freedom in Christ with discretion but never knowingly in a context that could lead weaker Christians to wrong conclusions.

Chapter 11—Commendation and reproof

Normally, good diplomacy offers commendation before reproof, and Paul was usually a good diplomat. Thus in chapter 11:2, the actual start of the chapter, Paul commended the Corinthians, perhaps in anticipation of the last half of the chapter, where he offered the negative counterpoint—"In the following [matters] I do not commend you" (17).

However, after this very brief commendation, he proceeded to instruct them regarding the complex issue of proper decorum in a public worship service. Throughout the first sixteen verses, Paul appears to fight on two fronts. On the one hand, some Corinthian women felt emancipated by the gospel and flaunted their newfound liberty. Others considered women as so inferior to men that they had no real place in public worship. So Paul had to dampen the overenthusiasm of the liberated women and at the same time try to prevent others from thinking of women as inferior.

Corinthian society kept women in a subservient relationship to men, with the result of widespread exploitation and prostitution. The gospel lifted women to a more noble position. However, the limits of their newfound freedom were not at all clear. For example, social custom called for women to wear veils whenever they went about in public areas, but the women of the Corinthian church had abandoned the veils when attending Christian meetings. Paul admonished them to dress for church in the same modest way they would dress when going about in the marketplace. Any other practice might be misconstrued as behavior unbecoming of respectable women. This chapter brings into focus the problem of making specific applications of broad principles. Here, the unchanging principle of proper worship decorum is clear, while the application of that principle (veiling of women; not cutting their hair) is subject to debate and change. In other words, female head-covering, whether by large amounts of hair or by a veil, has different meanings in different times and cultures. In first-century Corinth it was looked upon as an indication of female modesty. In more recent times, female modesty in the Western world has little connection with veils or long hair. Paul's larger principle is clear, however: In every time and culture, Christians should make every effort to present the cause of Christ as favorably as possible.

Paul's reproof in the second half of the chapter focuses on Corinthian practices relating to the Lord's Supper (20). Coupled with those practices was the same divisiveness he had scorned before (1:11; 3:5, 6, 22), only here it took on the nasty element of humiliating the poor (22). The exact nature of the meal is unclear. It appears to have had elements of a common meal ("Each one goes ahead with his own meal," verse 21), as well as elements of a ritual meal ("When you meet together, it is not the Lord's supper that you eat," verse 20). In fact, their behavior had so deteriorated that they had no concern for one another, for while "one is hungry . . . another is drunk." Such callousness is always inappropriate for Christian gatherings, but unspeakably so for something resembling the Lord's Supper.

Then, in the midst of his correctives, Paul reminded the Corinthians of what the Lord's table should mean to them. His language in verses 23-26 is highly familiar to many Christian groups today, who use the passage to introduce the celebration of the Lord's Supper. By his introductory phrase ("For I received from the Lord what I also delivered to you," verse 23), Paul apparently wanted to stress that the authority for this instruction was more than just his own. While Paul never considered his counsel frivolous or of little consequence, this introduction added thrust to his words. Clearly, the Lord's Supper was not to be just another meal—that they could do "at home" (34). But when they came together, their bread and drink were to help them "proclaim the Lord's death until he comes" (26).

Additional reading on chapter 6

1. Gordon D. Fee, *The First Epistle to the Corinthians, The New International Commentary on the New Testament,* ed. F. F. Bruce (Grand Rapids, Mich.: Eerdmans, 1987).
2. Ellen G. White, *The Acts of the Apostles,* pp. 309-317; 335-358.

Chapter

Seven

Spiritual Gifts
in Corinth

1 Corinthians 12-16

Chapter 12—The source and variety of spiritual gifts

The topic of spiritual gifts and religious enthusiasm nearly always stirs up heated discussion. As someone once said, "I don't know whether eating meat causes high blood pressure, but the discussion of it does." So also, it may not be clear whether spiritual gifts always cause emotional reactions, but the discussion of them does! And first-century Corinth proved no exception.

In verse 7 of the very first chapter of 1 Corinthians, Paul indicated that spiritual gifts were a matter of great interest among the Corinthian Christians: "You are not lacking in any spiritual gift." But then, after that brief observation, he immediately proceeded to reprove their divisiveness, suggesting that his reference to spiritual gifts at this point was tongue in cheek or even ironic. Whatever he meant to convey by the phrase, he simply dropped the subject throughout his first eleven chapters. But in chapter 12 he returned to the topic, and for the next three chapters he devoted more time and attention to spiritual gifts than to any other topic. Apparently the subject had caused lengthy (heated?) discussions, so Paul attempted to make things clear. For the Corinthians, he probably succeeded. But the historical and cultural distance between then and now, coupled with the ever-present problem of presuppositions, has resulted in a variety of interpretations. In fact, the spectrum of views on this topic is unusually broad, and the practices based on those views run the gamut from the sublime to the bizarre. Nevertheless, while some difficulties may always blur the picture slightly, we must attempt to make it as clear as we can.

In chapter 12:2 Paul indicated that some of the Corinthians, in their earlier state of paganism, had been jerked here and there "however you may have been moved." In other words, their actions were quite emotional in nature, and they probably did about anything they wanted to as long as some sense of "spirit" drove them. But now that they had come under the influence of a new Spirit, there was a limit to their offbeat behavior and expressions. It was preposterous, Paul asserted, to think that the Spirit would cause anyone to blaspheme the name of Christ by saying, "Jesus be cursed." To us, such admonition seems like such a given that it's almost absurd to even say it. But apparently the behavior of "spirit-led" pagans was occasionally extreme enough that Paul felt this counsel was credible. On the positive side, however, the confession, "Jesus is Lord" (3), can only be made sincerely by one who is Holy Spirit–directed.

In verses 4-11 Paul made only one really important point—the Holy Spirit is the source of a wide variety of equally important "gifts." Three times he used the word *varieties*—"*varieties* of gifts," "*varieties* of service," "*varieties* of working"—and each time he attributed them all to the same Spirit—Lord, or God. It was a crucial point for believers who might have admitted to a variety of gifts but were thoroughly convinced of a rigid hierarchy, with the gift of tongues at the top and the less spectacular ones like teaching or prophecy of much less interest. Paul spent considerable time amplifying this point in chapter 14, but in chapter 12, having stressed the divine origin of the various gifts, he illustrated their importance in verses 12-26. In fact, he thoroughly milked his analogy of the body and its parts (foot, ear, eye, etc.), of every drop of meaning until, the reader feels tempted to say, "Enough, enough! I get the point!" And what is the point? Simply this: Any human body has many diverse functions, all of which are absolutely necessary for the successful functioning of the body. The application is just as transparent—the church body must likewise have many different offices and gifts to function effectively. This message needed to be powerfully driven home, since the Corinthians had such a selective view of the hierarchy of gifts.

Accordingly, the stress of this body figure is on diversity first and unity second. Interpreters often invert these two or miss the first altogether. The point concerning unity is quite obvious—there is only one body, and its various parts must work harmoniously if the body is to work at all. That point needed to be made to a group that was fragmented into several factions. But equally important was the idea that a well-integrated body performs many functions with many parts, all of which are not only legitimate, but actually crucial to the proper functioning of the whole. The divisiveness in Corinth had resulted, at least in part, because each faction felt its hero or gift was the only necessary one. But a body in which certain functions are escalated at the expense of other necessary ones becomes crippled. Just as a body needs all its faculties, so a church needs a wide diversity of gifts to be successful.

At that point Paul addressed the mistaken notion that the less showy manifestations had less value. When he stated that "the parts of the body which seem to be weaker are indispensable. . . . But God has so composed the body, giving the greater honor to the inferior part," he was attempting to correct the Corinthian idea that certain spectacular spiritual gifts, such as glossolalia (tongue-speech), should be vigorously pursued, while others, such as apostleship, could be ignored or belittled. Thus Paul took their hierarchy of gifts, which had tongues at the top, and stood it on its head. It was therefore no accident, when he listed the gifts in verses 8-11 and 28-30, that in each case he put the gift of tongues at the bottom.

Paul concluded this line of reasoning in 12:27-30 by listing the gifts the Corinthians were most familiar with and then pointing out that no one gift had to be experienced by every member. This is clearly the meaning of his questions in

12:29, 30, "Are all prophets?" "Do all work miracles?" "Do all speak with tongues?" These rhetorical questions imply a negative answer. Put in the positive, Paul is saying, "All are not apostles or prophets or teachers. Nor do all possess the gift of healing or the gift of tongues." It was an important point for those who felt that tongue-speech was superior evidence of the Spirit's presence. In other words, the gifts of the Spirit are varied and are distributed according to God's perception of human needs, not merely on the basis of humans cultivating the right mental attitude or constructing just the right emotional environment.

Chapter 13—Love, the all-important motive

Paul concluded chapter 12 with an appeal that the Corinthians strive for the "higher gifts," but then he suggested that above all the gifts is the "more excellent way" of love. Though chapter 13 masterfully presents the many facets of "agape" love, it was not intended as an isolated essay. In fact, it is integral to Paul's reasoning regarding the Corinthian fixation with spiritual gifts. Paul here sets forth love as one of the two principal motives that should control the use of spiritual gifts. The other one is summed up in the word *edification,* which he used repeatedly in chapter 14 to show the superiority of prophecy to tongue-speech. Thus, while love is the ideal motive behind all Christian action, Paul here sets it forth as that which alone can validate any and all spiritual gifts. Or, to put it negatively, without love as the actuating agent, spiritual gifts in general are null and void, and glossolalia is nothing more than meaningless noise.

Chapter 14—The enigma of Corinthian tongue-speech

The issue of glossolalia (tongue-speech) in this chapter has given rise to extensive discussion and debate. The attention has focused on definitions of the phenomenon, the two most common of which are: (1) The phenomenon is a sudden ability to speak a language one has never studied; (2) it is a feeling of religious enthusiasm that expresses itself in audible vocalization comprised of no known language. Pentecostal churches usually adopt the second of these definitions.

Inasmuch as the experience of Pentecost described in Acts 2 comports with the first definition, many have assumed that Paul had in mind either that same phenomenon or an abuse of that phenomenon. But the language with which he described the Corinthian experience does not seem to fit the Pentecost experience. The following points in the Corinthian context speak more strongly in favor of ecstatic tongues than of xenoglossia, or foreign-language speech.

1. In verse 2 Paul clearly stated that the glossolalist "speaks not to men but to God," suggesting that the point of the experience is not human communication, but communication between the person and God, hence, a prayerlike experience.

2. Also in verse 2, Paul added that if a person did speak in tongues with others present, no one would understand him. While the Greek word Paul used here for *understand* actually means "hear," scholars overwhelmingly favor the idea that Paul used the term in this instance as a synonym for *understand*. In any case, no communication took place.

3. The last phrase of verse 2 makes clear that the problem was not with the ears of those listening but with the sounds of the one speaking—"He utters mysteries in the Spirit." This also indicates that there is something mystical about it all. Paul simply would not say it like this if the person were speaking German to people who only understood Latin. There would be nothing mystical about that.

4. In verses 3, 4 Paul stated the reason he preferred prophecy over tongues: Prophecy helps the speaker and his hearers, while tongues only help the speaker. Once again, the statement that glossolalia edifies only the speaker suggests that it is some sort of prayerlike experience which others do not enter into unless an interpretation is given. It is difficult to see how the phrase in verse 4, "edifies himself," would apply if the person involved were simply speaking in a foreign language.

5. The music illustrations Paul gave in verses 7, 8 focus on confused notes rather than on uneducated hearers. The notes are indistinct, not the hearing of the listeners. The distortion is in the sound of the instrument, not in the way

that sound is perceived. If Paul had had in mind distorted perception (someone talks in Spanish, but no one present understands Spanish), he might have used the analogy of an orchestra that performed flawlessly, but the audience was made up of deaf people. Paul seems to have had in mind a flawed transmitter rather than a flawed receiver.

6. In verses 10, 11 Paul set forth another analogy, this time referring to how communication fails when hearers do not understand the language of the speaker. Here the very scenario we have just described is the issue in Paul's mind—someone speaking a language unknown to all the hearers present. The surprising thing in these verses is Paul's change of vocabulary. Throughout this chapter, whenever Paul referred to the Corinthian tongue problem, he consistently used the Greek phrase *glossais lalein* ("to speak with tongues"), but in these two verses, and only in these two verses, when obviously referring to a foreign language, he used the Greek words *gene phonoi* ("kinds of sounds, languages"). Why the sudden change of terms? The simplest answer is that the analogy of a "foreign language" problem that Paul used in verses 10, 11 differed from the tongues problem among the Corinthians. Thus Paul used the illustration of languages (*phonoi*) as another way to make his point about "failed communication" (*glossais lalein*). To put it another way, it would be strange indeed for Paul to use an unknown foreign language (10, 11) to illustrate the problem of an unknown foreign language. The Corinthian problem had to be somehow different from what he described in verses 10, 11, or the illustration would have been foolishly redundant.

7. The counsel in verse 13 to pray for the power to interpret fits ecstatic speech more easily than it does a foreign language. The one who receives the gift of a foreign language, presumably to communicate the gospel, is at once bilingual. After all, he needs to know what he is saying as soon as he has said it so he can correct himself and possibly answer questions in the gift language. In that case, a separate gift of interpretation would be very strange. But if the gift is one of ecstatic tongues, then the speaker will always need the separate gift of interpretation to make known the meaning of his experience.

8. The reference in verse 14 to an unfruitful mind is mystifying if Paul was speaking of a foreign-language phenomenon because he equated tongue-speech with a state that he called an "unfruitful mind." If one could suddenly speak Latin fluently enough to proclaim the gospel to people in Rome, is it likely that he would simultaneously have diminished mental activity? Surely not. On the other hand, if the tongues phenomenon were an emotional experience, primarily at the feeling level, then some reference to a diminished mental state might not be so strange.

9. Also in verses 13, 15 Paul equated the phrase "speaks in a tongue" with "pray with the spirit." Such an interchange is not surprising in the light of verse 2, where he already equated speaking with a tongue with speaking to God (which was surely another way of describing a prayer experience). At the same time, the phrase "my spirit prays" would be a strange choice of words to describe a miraculous ability to understand and speak in a language different from one's mother tongue.

10. In verse 18 Paul said that he spoke with tongues even more than the Corinthians. One is immediately reminded of Paul's extensive travel throughout areas where different dialects were spoken, suggesting that this verse refers to several languages of the day. However, the word *more* in this verse is an adverb, which modifies the verb *speak*. If Paul had been describing the various languages he spoke, he would have used the word in its adjective form as a modifier of the word *tongues*. But he did not say that he spoke with "more tongues." Rather, he spoke "in tongues more." The stress is on the frequency of the experience rather than the multiplicity of tongues. Admittedly, this does not define the nature of the experience. It simply corrects the notion that "more tongues" might refer to a variety of commonly known foreign languages.

11. In verse 19 Paul hastened to add that his tongues experience was not something he did in church. His language is quite clear: When others are to be instructed, "five words with my mind" are far better than ten thousand "tongue" words, because during tongue-speech, the speaker's mind

remains inactive. So, if Paul spoke in tongues more than the excitable Corinthians, yet refrained from doing so while instructing others, we are forced to conclude that for Paul, the tongues experience must have been kept private.

12. In verse 21 Paul referred to the passage in Isaiah 28:11, 12, where the prophet foretold a calamity soon to befall the nation of Judah. Isaiah described a time when the people of Judah would hear strange "tongues" in the city because the invasion by the Babylonians would bring a "strange tongue" into Jerusalem, but in spite of that, some in Judah would continue to be unresponsive. Paul did not mean that a foreign language was again in evidence in Corinth. He was showing the stubbornness of unbelief and suggesting that such people needed some spectacular demonstration of power before they would believe. In that sense, people who were slow to believe needed the "sign" of tongues. This verse does not help us understand the nature of the tongues phenomenon. Rather, it gives us a glimpse into the mind-set of those who felt they needed such an experience.

13. In verses 23-25 Paul again turned to the current practices in Corinth and asserted that the noisy and disorderly way the Corinthian Christians used tongues was disastrous to unbelievers. It made them think the Christians were insane. In contrast, prophecy brings intelligible instruction, which can be used by the Holy Spirit to convict and convert. Plainly, Corinthian tongues were not an asset for the conversion of "outsiders," which would seem strange indeed if the church members were imbued with the ability to speak various languages. In the city where nationalities of East and West often met, a visitor happening upon the worship service would have been duly impressed if he had heard his mother tongue being used to tell the Christian story. Even if a certain amount of confusion reigned, if the phenomenon was a demonstration of foreign-language prowess, giving evidence that the speaker either possessed or was possessed by the Spirit, an unbelieving visitor, hearing his own home dialect, would hardly level the charge of insanity. But if several members simultaneously vocalized unintelligible syllables, the charge of insanity would be quite appropriate.

A plausible definition

Having said all of the above, a precise definition of ecstatic tongues is still difficult to spell out. For one thing, Paul never defined his terms. He assumed (correctly so) that his readers understood what he referred to. But his language was precise only in spelling out the abuse he attempted to correct. He did not clarify the nature of the genuine gift that lay behind the Corinthian abuses. Furthermore, Christian writings since the New Testament show that tongues experiences, whatever their nature, ceased and remained absent throughout most of Christian history. Not until the nineteenth century did a tongues phenomenon reemerge. Consequently, one should be cautious about equating today's Pentecostal-type tongues phenomenon with any biblical experience, since the entire phenomenon disappeared for some eighteen centuries.

Nevertheless, we need some definition of the Corinthian gift in order to benefit from Paul's counsel. In spite of the problems caused by the Corinthian practices, Paul never called for the phenomenon to be abolished. He only wanted it carefully regulated. Consequently, behind the obvious abuses in Corinth, there must have been an authentic gift that Paul consistently included in his lists of *charismata* (gifts of grace).

Given the preceding interpretation of chapter 14, it appears that the Corinthian glossolalia could be likened to a personal experience of prayer and praise brought about by the divine Spirit impressing the human spirit. The result was an emotional feeling of joy and peace, which Paul found difficult to put into words. It occasionally burst forth in rapturous expressions (like "hallelujah," perhaps) that needed "interpretation" before anyone else could fully benefit from the reasons behind such ecstaticism. Since the gift of "interpretation" was not automatic, God originally intended the tongues gift to be a private experience. As such, it gave scattered, personal evidences that the Spirit was present and thus encouraged and uplifted individuals. But given the Corinthian desire for excitement (14:12, "You are eager for manifestations of the Spirit"), the Lord provided a gift of "interpretation" by which the meaning of the private tongues experience could later be shared with the church. Unfortunately, since it, like the gift of healing, was a rather "showy" display, it soon became tainted with elements of pride that well-nigh obliterated any good that attended the original gift.

It is not always clear to Christians in other eras, with different backgrounds, why such manifestations of enthusiasm were so attractive to the Corinthians. At this point, it is helpful to keep in mind that the Corinthian believers had, for years, been surrounded by an atmosphere of pagan religions in which worship rituals were often extremely frenzied and ecstatic. Christians who had come out of such a background would be more prone to religious enthusiasm than Christians who had had little contact with religious ecstasy. Accordingly, since the Lord consistently tailors His methods of revelation to the differing needs of people, He allowed the Corinthians to experience a gift of tongues that met their individual needs.

But the conditions in Corinth that made tongues a meaningful gift for them may or may not exist in another Christian era. Paul gave no unequivocal statement that his lists of gifts were exhaustive for the rest of Christian history. In fact, the gift of apostleship must have been limited to the first century. Thus the demands by some Christians that all should speak in tongues or the insistence by others that no one should are equally wrong. It should also be remembered that the gift of tongues can easily be imitated, especially by a person who feels pressured to conform to a community expectation that the truly spiritual person will have some spontaneous experience to prove his spirituality. Still, the risk of abuse did not cause Paul to call for the abolishment of the gift—only its regulation.

The regulations

In verses 26-33 Paul set forth the regulations that, if followed, would make the tongues experience an acceptable part of Christian worship in Corinth. In fact, these six verses clearly summarize Paul's reasoning throughout the earlier part of the chapter. First, in contrast with the chaotic worship scene described in the first part of verse 26, Paul repeated the general principle of "edification" as that which must guide their worship practices. Here he plainly meant that concern for the good of the group must take precedence over the individual desire for display. Thus, tongue-speech could only be practiced if it was done one at a time, with an interpretation given for each, and not more than three such testimonies in any one meeting. Paul did not intend such regulations as an indirect way of abolishing tongues, for if he had felt they were completely wrong, he would have said so. Rather, these directives allowed the Corinthians to bring very personalized experiences into their worship services, but in an orderly manner that brought glory to God while not offending the uninitiated.

Chapter 15—The resurrection of Christ guarantees the resurrection of the saints

The interest generated by tongues in chapter 14 has tended to diminish the interest of modern readers in chapter 15, but this chapter on the resurrection is one of the most valuable in the whole epistle. According to Paul, this topic is of such magnitude that the gospel stands or falls with it (14, 15). To combat the heretical notion that Christ had not risen, Paul listed six appearances of Christ after His resurrection (5-8), some of which were to prominent leaders whose testimony should be accepted. Paul was so certain of the resurrection that he made no room for a Christianity without it, but reasoned in verse 19 that those who only have hope in this life are "most to be pitied."

Verse 29 is very difficult to interpret. Paul referred to some people being baptized "on behalf of the dead." But if baptism were meant to link the believer with the crucified and resurrected Christ (Rom. 6:4), then proxy baptism would surely have been unacceptable to Paul. Therefore, how and why did he refer to the practice? Many suggestions have been offered, but the most likely is that he was using an *argumentum ad hominem*—he used a practice or idea, well-known among his hearers, to lead them to a conclusion they would not have anticipated. He did not have to agree with the practice he cited since he only used it for purposes of illustration. Paul used the heretical practice of baptism for the dead to illustrate how widespread was the belief in some sort of resurrection. Without endorsing the practice, Paul may have been saying something like, "Even pagans and heretics fasten their faith on the hope of a resurrection, and if they cherish that hope, how much more should we!" (*SDA Bible Commentary*, vol. 6, p. 807). While the fine points of interpretation are open to debate, the primary point is clear: Even the practices of unbelievers add logical weight to the argument in favor of the resurrection.

Chapter 16—The final salutations

Chapter 16 is made up of Paul's final salutations, with a few admonitions thrown in. He began with an appeal for an offering for those in Jerusalem who had been suffering and then made reference to his plan to visit Corinth in the near future. After a few words of counsel, he wrote a final greeting in his own hand.

His brief reference in verse 2 to the first day of the week is not evidence that Christians at that time worshiped on Sunday. His emphasis was on systematic planning so the members would be prepared with an offering when he visited them.

Additional readings on chapter 7

1. D. A. Carson, *Showing the Spirit: A Theological Exposition of 1 Corinthians 12-14* (Grand Rapids, Mich.: Baker, 1987).

2. Gordon D. Fee, *The First Epistle to the Corinthians, The New International Commentary*, ed. F. F. Bruce (Grand Rapids, Mich.: Eerdmans, 1987).

3. Wyane Grudem, *The Gift of Prophecy in the New Testament and Today* (Westchester, Ill.: Crossway, 1988).

4. John Coolidge Hurd, Jr., *The Origin of 1 Corinthians* (New York: Seabury, 1965).

5. James Moffatt, *The First Epistle of Paul to the Corinthians, The Moffatt New Testament Commentary* (London: Hodder and Stoughton, 1939).

6. *SDA Bible Commentary*, vol. 6, pp. 653-818.

7. Ellen G. White, *The Acts of the Apostles*, pp. 317-322.

Chapter
Eight

God Sustains Those Who Suffer

2 Corinthians

Misery loves company" is a shallow cliché. Never-theless, when we are hurting, if we talk about it to anyone, we usually hope that that person can genuinely identify with our pain. Often it helps to know that the person has experienced something similar. Something like this must have been in Paul's mind as he sat down to write 2 Corinthians. He spoke here so frequently of his own suffering for the gospel that he must have felt it would serve to encourage other sufferers like himself.

Because this letter is designated *Second* Corinthians, it may seem of secondary importance when compared to First Corinthians. But while a smaller percentage of the letter is devoted to doctrinal instruction than is the case with 1 Corinthians, Paul's personal concern, even his agony over the spiritual well-being of the group, is perhaps more in-tensely expressed in this letter than in his preceding epistle. If anxious concern is counted as part of its value, 2 Corin-thians is valuable indeed.

Occasion
After Paul wrote his first letter to the Corinthians, he became

concerned that his counsel had been a bit harsh—that instead of promoting healing, he might actually have caused further alienation. Also, as time went by, certain false teachers filtered into the Corinthian church and made various insinuations about his apostleship and teaching. Consequently, Paul was more than a little anxious to get some direct word from the church about how the members had received his counsels and what impact his enemies were having. He had sent the first letter by the hand of Titus and apparently had made arrangements to meet Titus afterward in Troas for a report. After a reasonable amount of time elapsed, Paul left Ephesus for Troas and his meeting with Titus. Titus failed to appear, so Paul traveled on westward into Macedonia, where he finally met up with Titus, possibly at Philippi. The report Titus brought was mixed. Consequently, Paul rejoiced over the good news (7:7-11) and grieved over the rest (10:10, 11). It is likely that he penned his reactions shortly after receiving the report from Titus in Philippi. How much time had gone by since the writing of 1 Corinthians is not clear, but it was surely not more than a few months. This would date the letter late in the year A.D. 57.

Purpose and theme

In 2 Corinthians, Paul's doctrinal instructions are brief—chapters 3 and 5—compared to his pastoral concerns. "Weakness, grief, peril, tribulation, comfort, boasting, truth, ministry, glory—these are some of the terms that stand out and serve to carry the thread of the thought" (Everett Harrison, *Introduction to the New Testament*, rev. ed. [Grand Rapids, Mich.: Eerdmans, 1977], p. 293). Because of these many pastoral concerns, the letter seems at first reading to lack any cohesive central idea. But many scholars believe that the underlying theme of the letter is Paul's suffering for the gospel and God's all-sufficient sustaining power. Such an account authenticates his apostolic calling, and at the same time it offers encouragement to those who will likewise suffer.

Chapters 1 and 2—Paul explains his conduct

In his greeting Paul made it clear that he intended this

letter to have a wide hearing—"to the church . . . with all the saints . . . in the whole of Achaia." In verses 3-11 he expressed one of the recurring themes of the letter—his thanksgiving, not just for deliverance *out of* affliction, but for comfort *in* affliction. That is important counsel for any who will, sooner or later, experience similar suffering and trials. We must all be prepared to endure, for there is no promise of deliverance from affliction. Instead, we must find comfort in the midst of our suffering. In fact, Paul used the key word *comfort* ten times in verses 3-7. Paul then stressed his point in verse 5 by stating that just as the sufferings for Christ increased, so the comfort increased proportionately.

But this opening section contains more than thanksgiving for God's sustaining comfort in affliction. Paul wanted to assure the Corinthians that, contrary to some accusations, his failure to visit them sooner was not due to fickleness on his part (1:17), but was a result of the severe affliction he had suffered in Asia—a hardship so great he had despaired of life itself (1:8). In other words, his devotion to them was total and his desire to visit them, sincere (1:12-14).

In chapters 1:15–2:13 Paul explained to the Corinthians the reasons why he had not visited them sooner. Not only had he suffered some limiting difficulty in Asia; he was also concerned that a premature visit would be unnecessarily painful (2:1). Apparently he wanted a little more time to elapse after they received his first letter, since some of his counsel had been rather caustic (1 Cor. 5:6-9). Admonition to disfellowship is usually divisive, so Paul probably hoped that, as time passed, the faithful members would do what was necessary to rectify the situation and then strive for unity. At the same time, he assured the Corinthian believers that his reproofs were prompted only by sincere love (2:4). Furthermore, he advised them that if decisive action against the chief offender had brought about genuine repentance, they were to reaffirm their love by showing forgiveness and acceptance. The implication in 2:13 is that Paul finally got good news from Titus, which caused him in 2:14-17 to express his thanks to God for the privilege of being God's "aroma" of salvation.

Chapter 3—Glory that fades and glory that lasts

In answer to the charge of certain critics that Paul's credentials were suspect, he asserted in chapter 3:1-3 that the Corinthian believers themselves were his best recommendation. A letter written with pen and ink can communicate ideas and even concern in a crisp, precise way, but a testimony given verbally by a concerned and loving person, followed by a consistent, real-life example, is of far greater weight and makes a much more lasting impression. So Paul appealed to the Corinthians to look around them for evidence of the genuineness of his message. You will see it much more easily in hearts and lives, he said in effect, than in words written on papyrus or even on "tablets of stone" (3).

Paul then used his analogy of pen and ink as a springboard to a higher level of theological reflection. In verse 6 he began drawing a contrast between the gospel as the new covenant, enlivened by the Spirit, and the written code, called a dispensation of death, that had only a fading splendor. In verses 7-18 Paul contrasted the Jewish system with the Christian message. Although giving the law to Israel through Moses began with such brilliance that the face of Moses shone, that system could not *of itself* bring a permanent splendor. In fact, to the extent that the Judaizers contented themselves with that system and rejected Christ, it became, not just a dispensation of fading glory, but dispensation of death. Life, freedom, and lasting glory can be found only in Christ. And the glory is not just a future hope. It starts at the very beginning of the Christian walk. Too often, all sense of *glory* (a strong word) is reserved for something yet to be—after we have finally developed into the kind of believers God approves. But Paul here described Christian growth as a gradual change from one degree of glory to another (18). Truly a law-book approach to religion compares terribly with the "glory" of being and growing in Christ.

Chapter 4—The final reward will far outweigh the present suffering

Always being on the defensive is a tiring, frustrating experience. In addition, when a person is defending himself, he is not doing anything new or creative. With that in mind, it is a wonder that Paul was able to accomplish as much as he did, since he was always having to defend himself. In the early verses of chapter 4, he again defended himself against the charges of his enemies. He asserted that his procedures had not been secretive or underhanded, and if there was any obscurity, the problem was with the hearers, not with his proclamation. Any veiling of the message had taken place only through the agency of the evil one, who had found fertile ground for his insinuations and doubts in the minds of "those who are perishing" (3). Here Paul clearly showed the ongoing battle that is taking place between the "god of this world" (4) and the God of our Lord Jesus Christ. And, while Christ's victory over sin had ensured Satan's ultimate defeat, there was not yet *total* victory, in that the reign of Christ over all had yet to be realized. In the interim, though darkness remained, a light now shone out of the darkness, which was the glory of God as seen in the face of our Lord Jesus Christ (6).

In verses 7-18 Paul returned to his familiar theme of suffering on behalf of the gospel and the power from heaven that makes perseverance possible. He did this by a series of paradoxes, which is typical of this epistle and of his own style. The first contrast in verse 7 points out the great value Paul placed upon the message ("this treasure") and the apparent worthlessness of the ministers of that message ("earthen vessels"; "clay pots," TEV). This contrast served as an answer to those critics who had charged that Paul was weak in body and speech (10:1, 10). He admitted that although those "vessels" were fragile clay pots, the message they contained was priceless, nonetheless. Furthermore, although he suffered intensely, he felt rewarded by the thought that his hardship was simply part of the cost of making Christ known to the Corinthian believers. In fact, he seems to suggest a kind of proportionality—the more he experienced suffering and hardship for Christ, the richer was the experience of the Corinthian believers in the Christian walk (10-12). And in addition to their deepening faith, that which held Paul steadfast through affliction was his faith in the resurrection and the glory of the future life (17, 18).

Chapter 5—Life with Christ is superior to life in this world

In chapter 5 Paul brought up the possibility of his own death before the second advent of Christ. Previously, he had implied that he would be among the living at the last trump (1 Thess. 4:17; 1 Cor. 15:51, 52). Now, having just stressed in chapter 4 the fragile nature of the physical body, he went a step further and raised the specter of his own death. The figure he used for the body—a tent—was natural for a tentmaker. Following the theme of chapter 4, Paul suggested that life in this tent was characterized by groaning and anxiety (2-4), so it was natural to desire the better life that God had prepared. He hoped to avoid the state of being naked, which he equated with death.

Paul's words in verses 6-8 about being "away from the body and at home with the Lord" have led some to conclude that Paul taught a conscious existence in death. But such a conclusion is not warranted, either by this immediate context or by Paul's overall teaching. In this passage, Paul had stressed the hardship of his life in this tent, or body. Accordingly, he quite naturally expressed his longing for that time when such affliction would be over and he would be with the Lord. Being away from the body was simply Paul's way of saying away from the sufferings and trouble that characterize this physical life. That the state he desired was not death is clear from his repeated wish, expressed in verses 3, 4, that he not be unclothed. In an earlier letter, he had assured the grieving Thessalonians that those who died before the second coming will not precede the living saints into the presence of Christ (1 Thess. 4:15, 16), but rather, the two groups will meet in the clouds simultaneously at the last trump. In the meantime, although still "away from the Lord" in body, they were to be "of good courage" (6). Nevertheless, when pressures mount and despair looms, what struggling Christian does not echo Paul's desire to be away from all this and "at home with the Lord"?

Paul's entire message and mission is wonderfully encapsulated in the last six verses of chapter 5. In verse 17 he described the Christian as a "new creation," not just a moderately reeducated Jew. Then he emphasized the grace element by stating that "all this is from God, who through Christ reconciled us to himself." That, of course, was the crux of Paul's preaching and teaching. He concluded with his statement of mission: God not only reconciled us, but made us ambassadors of that message of reconciliation. God now makes His appeal to others through us. Nowhere else is Paul's message and mission summarized so clearly and succinctly.

Chapters 6-9

Chapter 6 contains additional words of encouragement in the face of difficulties. Chapter 7:8-13 speaks of an attitude of repentance that probably had a direct bearing on the Corinthian congregation's treatment of the incestuous member first referred to in 1 Corinthians 5. It seems clear that they had repented of their arrogance (1 Cor. 5:2, 6); had cleaned up the church, probably by disfellowshiping the man ("what zeal, what punishment," verse 11); and had returned to the good graces of both Paul and Titus (7:15, 16). Chapters 8 and 9 relate to the collection for the poor in Jerusalem and Paul's desire that the Corinthians would be generous.

Chapters 10-13—Paul's harsh admonitions

In chapter 10 Paul introduced a sudden change of tone. In the preceding nine chapters he tossed an occasional barb at his Judaizing enemies, but in these last four chapters his warnings and reproofs were unsparing. The change in emphasis has been explained in various ways, but no commentator denies the shift. Explanations vary from a pause in his dictating to a sudden mood swing on Paul's part.

While he continued to address the church in general, he directed his sternest remarks in these chapters toward those implacable Judaizers who continued their false teachings and false charges. Among other things, they had attacked Paul's apostolic authority by suggesting that he was only firm in his words when he was absent from them. His "bodily presence is weak" (10:10). Paul jumped on that notion with great vigor. In the process, his admonitions ran the gamut from friendly cajoling ("I wish you would bear with me in a little foolishness," 11:1) to ominous charges that his enemies were Satan's agents (11:15).

If one central theme runs throughout these last four chapters, it is Paul's defense of his apostleship. He did this in chapter 10 by reminding the Corinthians that he had been the first to bring them the message (14). In chapter 11 he called to mind the extended hardships he had suffered in the process of carrying out his apostolic calling (23-29). No one has suffered more torture or brushes with death for the sake of Christ, so his enemies' charges that he was self-serving were patently false.

In chapter 12:1-5 he referred to a vision that had been part of the divine input in his life. Although he spoke of it as though it were someone else ("I know a man in Christ"), most scholars assume he was referring to a personal experience. At any rate he used that mysterious happening as a part of his "boast" that his calling was genuine. In this same context he also referred to his much-debated "thorn . . . in the flesh" (7-9). The fact that the Lord did not see fit to remove this "messenger of Satan" added weight to his earlier argument that his mission was not driven by selfish motives. Not only did he fail to get rich from the gospel; he continued to pay a heavy price to carry out his mission. The conclusion to which this extended defense leads is simple: Because Paul's apostleship was indeed genuine, the Corinthians could ignore his various admonitions only at their peril.

Additional reading on chapter 8

1. Murray J. Harris, *2 Corinthians, The Expositor's Bible Commentary,* ed. Frank E. Gaebelein (Grand Rapids, Mich.: Zondervan, 1976).
2. Philip E. Hughes, *Paul's Second Epistle to the Corinthians, The New International Commentary on the New Testament* (Grand Rapids, Mich.: Eerdmans, 1962).
3. *SDA Bible Commentary,* vol. 6, on 2 Corinthians.
4. Ellen G. White, *The Acts of the Apostles,* pp. 323-334.

Chapter
Nine

The Letter of Liberty
Galatians

Paul's epistles suggest that his enemies were many and their masks diverse. They appeared on every horizon, always dedicated to the one goal of giving Paul the reverse of encouragement. In the letter to the Galatians, Paul seemed unusually vexed by them and determined to answer their charges and neutralize their influence. These Judaizing Christians had attempted to create a hybrid religion by combining elements of Judaism with Christianity. They held strongly to a concept of merit righteousness. After Paul proclaimed to the Galatian believers the importance of faith in Christ, they replied, "Fine, believe in Christ, but be sure to practice the necessary rituals as well." To which Paul responded, "Wrong! To *add* anything to Christ as essential for salvation is to nullify the freedom of the gospel."

The recipients—who and where?

While the message of the book of Galatians seems clear, the location and identity of the recipients poses some difficulty. Whereas Paul directed letters such as Thessalonians and Corinthians to Christians located in well-known cities, he directed the letter to the Galatians to a region, not a city, and even the region is not precisely located. Furthermore, maps of the area provide little help, since the region of Galatia had different boundaries at different times. In the third century B.C., Galatia was a relatively small territory in northern Asia Minor (modern Turkey), inhabited by the Gauls. By 25 B.C., the Romans had come to power, had conquered this region, and had expanded its borders south to the Mediterranean Sea. Thus, in Paul's time, Galatia included the territory around Iconium, Lystra, and Derbe— all cities far to the south of the original Galatia, which Paul had visited on his first missionary journey. The question is whether in his letter Paul had in mind Galatia in its earlier, restricted sense, or in its later, Roman sense that included the cities of the south.

The language of Luke in Acts favors the northern, smaller region, as he referred to the southern cities of Lystra and Derbe as "cities of Lycaonia" (Acts 14:6) and Antioch as part of Pisidia (Acts 13:14). He did not mention Galatia in this context. On the other hand, when he described the northern itinerary of the second journey, Luke called the region Galatia (Acts 16:6). This area was quite distinct from the previously mentioned regions. While the issue cannot be resolved with certainty, we will accept the language of Luke and conclude that the letter to the Galatians was addressed to believers in the northern section of Asia Minor, through which Paul traveled on his second and possibly third missionary journeys.

Date

The conclusion that the Galatians lived in the north puts certain limits on dating the letter. It is clear from Paul's letter that he had previously visited the community and preached there. If the region involved was in the south, the letter could have been written anytime after the first missionary journey. But if Paul was writing to Christians in the north, then the letter could not have been written until sometime during or after the second missionary journey. Furthermore, the references in 1:9 and 4:13 to his preaching to them "at first" have been interpreted by some to mean that Paul had been through Galatia twice before. While this issue cannot be resolved with certainty, the language of Luke, coupled with the similarity of content between Romans and Galatians, has suggested to many scholars that the two books were both written during Paul's three-month stay in Corinth during his third missionary journey. If so, the date would be A.D. 57/58.

The charges

The letter focuses on three charges against Paul and his teachings. First, his enemies claimed that he was not a true apostle. Since he was not one of the twelve, he lacked that which was absolutely essential for credibility—complete acceptance by the twelve. Paul responded by recounting the highlights of his past that bore directly on his apostolic calling. He told of his change from persecuting Pharisee to believing Christian in such a way as to show clearly that the entire experience was masterminded by the One who "had called me through his grace" (1:15). Personal ambition and human initiative had nothing whatever to do with his conversion. In addition, he defended his authority by setting forth his independence from the apostles ("I did not confer with flesh and blood," verse 16), thereby indicating that his authority equaled the authority of the twelve.

Of course, if Paul's apostolic authority was called into question, so also was the accuracy of his message. His enemies charged him with preaching a flawed gospel, which conveniently set aside all law keeping for Christians. Paul insisted that human righteousness is not determined by a relationship to law but by a faith relationship to Christ. Exhibit A of this truth, he said, is Abraham, whom God reckoned righteous before the law was given, and even before he was circumcised.

Finally, Paul's enemies charged that his gospel led to moral recklessness. They claimed that the logical outcome of his preaching was antinomianism (lawlessness) and loose living. But Paul undercut this charge by warning that Christians should not use their newfound freedom as an "opportunity for the flesh" (5:13, 16), but should recognize that with conversion comes a tension between the flesh and the Spirit. He then added the warning that yielding to the desires of the flesh will result in missing out on the kingdom of God (5:21). Contrary to the charge, his gospel implied serious devotion.

Chapter 1—Paul's apostolic qualifications

The opening words of this letter reflect the leading charge of Paul's enemies: His apostolic authority was suspect. Accordingly, he was not content to refer to himself as "an apostle." Rather, he traced his apostolic calling to both Jesus Christ and God the Father. In addition, he underscored his independence from the other apostles by stating that his apostleship came "not from men nor through man." He returned to this theme repeatedly throughout the letter, but he especially emphasized it in chapters 1 and 2.

In most of his letters, after his initial salutation, Paul added some words of thanks or commendation for the faith and practice of his readers. However, this is missing in Galatians. Apparently Paul felt that the heresy was so serious and the need for correction so urgent that no word of praise was warranted. His words sound harsh and unsparing, and they carried weight, since he based them on conviction rather than on wounded personal pride.

In verses 6-9 Paul gave the primary reason he felt so distressed: The gospel he had proclaimed to the Galatians was being corrupted. This hurt Paul far more than personal slander. His pride might suffer from a personal attack, but little else. But when the gospel was undermined, it affected the salvation of others, and that was disaster. That's why his language was so much more severe in Galatians than in any of his other letters. Never one to understate his case, Paul pronounced a curse on anyone, human or angel, who might have the audacity to preach a gospel that differed in any significant way from that which he had preached.

Beginning with verse 11, Paul refuted the specific charges of his opponents. Since they were questioning the viability of his calling, he had to begin there. He reviewed the journey he had taken from zealous Pharisee to Christian evangelist. Although he did not enumerate the details of his conversion experience as he later did for the Jews in Jerusalem (Acts 22:6-11) and for Agrippa and Festus (Acts 26:12-18), he made clear that the impetus for this incredible change of direction all came from God. In fact, he added the thought that it was all in the mind of God before he was born (15)!

Surely no man so zealous for the Jewish faith ("I advanced in Judaism beyond many of my own age," verse 14) would have been converted by any human devising. Paul then underscored both his independence and his authority by asserting that he did not "confer with flesh and blood" (16). His departure to Arabia for three years (17, 18) showed conclusively that he spent this formative period as a Christian far from human counsel.

The sequence of events given here in Galatians does not harmonize readily with that in Acts 9, where Luke had Paul going directly from his conversion experience to the synagogue to preach (Acts 9:20). When trouble developed, he moved straight from Damascus to Jerusalem, where Barnabas convinced the skeptical apostles to accept the newly converted Paul. Luke made no mention of an Arabian sojourn or of a longer period (fourteen years, Gal. 2:1) of relative obscurity prior to Paul's full fellowship with the apostles.

The greater detail of the Galatians account, coupled with the fact that it is an autobiography, argues for its reliability. The account in Acts is not wrong, simply incomplete. Writing to his friend Theophilus, Luke wanted to show the spirit of unity that existed among the apostles in those early times. Consequently, he gave few details between Paul's conversion and his reconciliation with the twelve. Paul, on the other hand, needed to establish his authority and independence— a concern that in this instance outweighed the issue of unity. That is why he stressed his independence from the twelve so strongly at the beginning of his letter.

Chapter 2—Paul and the church authorities

Having established his apostolic credentials in chapter 1, in 2:1-10 Paul showed that in time, an essential unity developed between himself and the other apostles. He recounted the meeting in Jerusalem when he laid before the apostles "who were of repute" (2) the essence of his gospel. Since he earlier mentioned that fourteen years had elapsed (1), this meeting was probably the Jerusalem Council of A.D. 49, which Luke described in fuller detail in Acts 15. Paul's purpose for laying his message before the apostles was probably not to secure their approval of what he preached. Even though in verse 2 he expressed fear that he might have run in vain, he was not uncertain about the accuracy of his gospel. Such a thought would have been irreconcilable with his repeated statements in chapter 1:8, 9 that even angels could not correct his message. Paul's fear was more likely that the Judaizers had influenced the apostolic leaders to such an extent that they might seek to hinder his evangelistic endeavors.

At this point Paul had to deal with three distinct philosophies or parties. First, there was his own view, which included receiving the Gentiles as Christians without requiring them to accept Mosaic rules such as circumcision. Second, there were the "false brethren," who contended that all Gentiles must be circumcised as a sign of their commitment. Finally, there were those, some in positions of leadership, who were being influenced one way or the other by the first two groups. In the midst of such contention for influence, Paul was understandably pleased when, having made Titus a test case against the necessity of circumcision, he won. Further, he reported with some satisfaction that the outcome of the discussion with those "who were of repute" necessitated no changes in either his message or his methods. They "added nothing to me" (6).

In verses 11-16 Paul went a step beyond asserting his equality with the "pillar apostles," Peter and Barnabas. He recalled with considerable detail the incident concerning the "circumcision party," where he had publicly corrected Peter for his flagrant double standard ("I withstood him to the face," KJV). Over and above the fact of that incident stands the written record. In other words, it was one thing for Paul to publicly correct and humble Peter for his hypocrisy, but another thing to write to some mutual friends about it. Paul took this unusual step, not only to make sure the Galatians properly understood the gospel, but also to enhance his own standing as an apostle. After all, not just anyone could correct the *chief* apostle, Peter.

Verses 15-21 contain not only the primary burden of the epistle, but also the primary truths of the gospel. At some point here, Paul's remarks to Peter ended and his instruction for the church at large resumed, but the precise point of that transition is not clear. In any case, verse 16 is crucial, in that it contains the first occurrence of the contrasting ideas, "justified by faith" and "works of the law." Here Paul used the term *justify* in its forensic sense of "to acquit." The word often carries a great deal of theological freight, but here it simply refers to the proclamation by God that the guilty are acceptable to Him. That acceptability is based, not on any previous goodness, or even on the exercise of faith. It is simply the demonstration of God's grace, and faith is the human response of acceptance of that grace. So when God's free *grace* impacts on a person's consciousness and that person extends the hand of *faith* to receive it, God then imputes Christ's righteousness to the believer. At this point in the process, human works play absolutely no role. Whatever historical figure Paul cited—Abraham or David or even himself—the message was always the same—God acquitted that person before he had done any good works. Here Paul pounded home the importance of the issue by repeating the "justified by faith" concept three times in verse 16 alone.

At the same time, Paul used the noun *righteousness* and the verb *justify—to declare* righteous—to refer to conformity to the divine requirement. But if "to declare righteous" is nothing more than God calling sinners "not guilty," then a kind of legal fiction is involved when God justifies a person. To put it another way, if God treats a justified person "just-as-if" he had never sinned, then pretense is in there somewhere. That person has, in fact, sinned, and everybody knows it. To simply acquit him says nothing at all about his moral rectitude. If "conformity to the divine requirement" includes anything at all about moral behavior, justification at this level simply doesn't address it. But how can God justify Himself while justifying sinners?

In Romans 3:25, 26 Paul approached this very question, but his answer there is too brief to be satisfying. He simply states that Christ's sacrificial death gives evidence of God's righteousness when He declares righteous the person who has faith in Jesus. Or as the KJV nicely puts it, He is "just, and the justifier." In that context he said nothing further about human response or behavior. But elsewhere, Paul spoke a great deal about the *life* of the believer and suggested that such a life should begin to assimilate and reflect divine characteristics. Thus, in Galatians 5:13 he warned against the possibility that the believer might use his freedom in Christ "as an opportunity for the flesh." In contrast, he asserted that the Christian life will be characterized by the fruits of the Spirit, which are love, joy, peace, patience, kindness, etc. So there is a connection between being declared righteous and right behavior. In fact, Paul would probably say that when a person is declared righteous, he really is so, not in the sense that he is perfect, but in the sense that his direction has changed, and a new power is at work in his life. Such changes may appear subtle or insignificant, but they clearly indicate that a whole new person has come into being (Eph. 2:15). By God's grace and decree, the believer's *status* has changed dramatically—from lost to justified—and by that same grace, his *behavior* has begun to change. In summary, the forensic idea of "acquit" is only the initial aspect of right standing with God. To put it another way, a *life* of faith follows the *act* of faith. While Paul stressed the latter, he did not ignore the former.

The charge that Paul's theory of justification by faith dangerously eliminated all need for law and thus destroyed all sense of moral responsibility was logical but, according to Paul, unwarranted. According to the charge, since the believers continued in sin, Christ was thereby made indirectly responsible for the state of continued sin. Without explanation, Paul abruptly dismissed this notion by saying, in effect, "ridiculous." Then in verse 18 he explained that if he should "build up again" the things he had torn down, that is, turn again to a law-keeping approach after having come to Christ by faith, it would only result in his being proved a transgressor, a lawbreaker. But he asserted in verses 19, 20 that such could not be the case, for he had died to law, so he could not possibly return to it.

A favorite theme—the results of his union with Christ—springs out of 2:20. For Paul, that union was so tight that

Christ's death became his death, Christ's resurrection ensured his resurrection, and Christ's glorified life guaranteed
his glorified life.

Chapter 3—Law and faith explained

In chapters 1 and 2, Paul spoke largely out of his own
experience, but in chapters 3 and 4 he set forth his more
formal defense of the gospel. He addressed his hearers by the
rather somber term *Galatians* rather than the more intimate
brethren that he usually favored. In fact, his language was full
of pathos as he lamented their foolish gullibility for being so
easily dissuaded from the truth he had taught them. Paul
was incredulous that they could have such an exciting start
"with the Spirit" and such a dismal ending "with the flesh"
(3). Having been such a legalist himself, Paul could not
fathom how a legal, merit-righteousness could hold more
fascination than the gospel of freedom.

Among the Judaizers, Abraham was exhibit A of what
merit-righteousness looked like. He was the greatest of
obedient patriarchs. But in chapter 3:6-9 Paul upended their
comfortable concept by holding up Abraham as the prime
example of how God's initiating grace, apart from any good
works or other "conditions," made more feasible the salvation
of the Gentiles than could any form of works-righteousness.
"Men of faith" can be from any background, and such faith
makes them true heirs of Abraham, "who had faith" (9). Such
a concept leaves no room for a *required* circumcision or a law
(Jewish) background.

In the first nine verses of chapter 3, Paul discussed justification from the positive stance of the necessity of faith. In
verses 10-14 he turned to the negative side of the argument
to show the impossibility of justification by law. Not only
does the law not justify; it erects a standard of perfection that
no one can keep, so all human beings stand under its curse.
The only positive outcome is by default. The sense of futility,
aggravated by the law, drives people to the only solution,
which is Christ, who became the curse for us (13).

Paul got still more theological mileage out of Abraham's
example. In verses 15-18 he reminded the Galatians that

once a covenant or will is agreed to by both parties involved, it cannot be annulled or changed. Just so, God made a covenant in the form of promises with Abraham, which was ratified, that is, accepted, by Abraham. Then, 430 years later, God gave the law to Israel. But that giving of the law could not annul or in any way change the previously ratified covenant promises made to Abraham.

This, of course, calls for some explanation regarding the positive function of law, though it appears to come out with a rather negative twist: the law was given to accentuate and increase sin! Here Paul used the term *parabasis* for sin, which means a knowledgeable choosing to go against an express command. It seems intentional that he did not refer to this kind of sin as *hamartia,* which is more like an inadvertent falling short of expectations. In this sense, then, the law, though present in abstract form earlier, was made concrete at Sinai and became that which made sin stand out as rebellion against explicit, divine directives. So law made sin come out into the open and show itself as sin in all its rebelliousness. Still, there is a positive outcome to all this, and Paul explained that next. The coming of law and its subsequent enhancement of sin is the catalyst that brings about the confrontation with Christ, who is the solution (22).

This called for further clarification of the law's function. Here Paul seems to have been operating on two fronts. On the one hand, he addressed the issue of law before and after Christ's sacrifice in A.D. 31—a kind of historical approach. On the other hand, he made a spiritual application of the law's function in the life of a person before and after he comes to have faith in the sacrifice of Christ. Thus, since Christ ("faith") has come, there is no more need to live under the enslavement of the schoolmaster. In other words, the historical coming of Christ must be actualized in my experience if I am to be freed from the rule of the "custodian."

But what is this law that Paul likened to a "schoolmaster" (KJV), or "custodian" (RSV)? The *SDA Bible Commentary* (vol. 6, p. 961) emphasizes the ceremonial aspect of law as that which is best described as a "custodian." But the Greek word *paidagōgos* was used for a "child-supervisor," employed by wealthy Greeks to oversee their children. Such a servant was not considered a teacher or tutor, and he belonged only to the period of a child's immaturity. Paul stressed this point in chapter 4:1-7, where he equated childhood with slaves and guardians and being "under the law," and then contrasted that state with the state of sonship and becoming an heir.

So the figure of being "under the law" is a rich one. It no doubt refers to Israel prior to A.D. 31, but also to anyone who lives under the law and believes that careful living will somehow result in life eternal for the practitioner. Paul had been describing the functional but negative aspect of law as it drives the frustrated sinner to Christ and His salvation. From this perspective, Paul included, in chapter 3:24, not just the ceremonial laws of the sacrificial system of Israel, but also the Decalogue. It is that Ten-Commandment law which passes condemnation on the sinner, who finds perfect obedience just beyond his grasp. But for the sinner who accepts Christ's solution, the condemning law has done its work, and that work now ends.

But the law is too complex to dismiss so simply. While it passes judgment on sinners, it also stands as an objective guide for the believer. Yet even in this respect, the letter of the law is transcended when the author of that law comes to live in the believer. The word *transcend* here does not mean "destroy," but "bring to life" or "make more meaningful." For example, there may be rules that describe the limits of acceptable behavior for married people, but a loving relationship with a husband or wife "transcends" those rules.

So the law performs both a negative and a positive function. On the negative side, it stands as the divine ideal, which, combined with the weakness of the flesh (Rom. 8:3), condemns, but never justifies persons. The resulting sense of futility serves a positive function in leading the person to Christ. In this sense, the *condemning* aspect of the law ("custodian") is lifted when Christ comes into the life.

But a function of the law does continue after conversion— it remains as an objective guide. To say that the author of the law dwells within does not abolish the continuing usefulness of the law as a standard of behavior. But it no longer stands apart from a person on two tables of stone; it is written on the very fiber of his or her being, so that the righteous requirements of the law are fulfilled in the life of one who has Christ within. Accordingly, in chapter 4:6 Paul asserted that God has "sent the Spirit of his Son into our hearts."

For Paul, that "in Christ" experience was the great equalizer. The continuing debate about requirements before and after conversion and how those requirements differed for Jews and non-Jews was now moot. In Christ, distinctions disappear. In unequivocal language, Paul thrust home the point that there was now "neither Jew nor Greek . . . neither slave nor free . . . neither male nor female" (3:28). Equality of status could hardly be more strongly stated.

Chapter 4—Doctrinal instruction on law concluded

In chapter 4:21-31 Paul concluded the doctrinal portion of his letter by means of an allegory that seems a bit strained at certain points. To once more illustrate and contrast the law and the gospel, he drew from sacred history the account of Hagar, the bondwoman, and Sarah, the free woman. Paul used these women and their children to represent the contrasting positions of law and grace. Ishmael, born after the natural order of things, represented the old covenant of law—earthly Jerusalem and Judaism. In contrast, Isaac, whose birth was supernatural, stood for promise, the new covenant, the new Jerusalem, and Christianity. Having drawn the various analogies, Paul brought them into his time with some applications that are interesting, if not transparent. Thus, when he said, "We . . . like Isaac, are children of promise" (28), did he mean Jewish Christians, Gentile Christians, or just generic Christians, regardless of their background? And does "born according to the flesh" (29) refer to natural birth or to birth as a Jew, or does it mean refusal to accept the message of the gospel, since it is juxtaposed with "born according to the Spirit"? While all his figures are not easily explained, the general message is, as usual, quite clear—we are children characterized by freedom, not slavery.

Chapter 5—The life of freedom

In chapter 5:1-12 Paul directed all his fervor against the notion that circumcision was essential for salvation. But circumcision alone was not the issue. As Paul used the term, it represented the entire legalistic scheme being urged by the Judaizers. Circumcision was simply the prime example of a way of thinking. The rite itself was not bad; originally, it had served as a sign or seal of Abraham's faith (Rom. 4:11). In fact, it still could have meaning in that way. But it was not being touted that way by Paul's opponents in Galatia. They held up circumcision as absolutely binding on both Jewish and Gentile Christians. They taught that Christ and circumcision went together to make up the divine requirement. With vigorous language Paul denied that combination and said in 5:2 that it was Christ *or* circumcision, but it could not be both. Circumcision and all the legal rules it symbolizes play absolutely no role in our acceptance with God. It is not that a circumcised person cannot be saved, but that circumcision is not a condition for obtaining salvation. To hold any other view, Paul said, is to challenge the sufficiency of Christ's work.

Chapter 5:13–6:18—Responsibilities of freedom

In this last section of the letter, Paul addressed some ramifications of the life that has been set free in Christ. He acknowledged that the life of liberty must have some direction, or it may deteriorate from liberty to license. In short, Christian freedom does not do away with ethics and certain limits on behavior. Paul knew that, in terms of freedom, his gospel would come across to many law-oriented Jews as similar to the widespread pagan normlessness. Consequently, he issued his caution that freedom in Christ has limits— Christians should not use it as an "opportunity for the flesh" (5:13).

Paul first offered the controlling principles of service to others and love of one's neighbor (13, 14). He then explained that, although tension will continue between the Spirit and the flesh, the Christian led by the Spirit (16) will not be a slave to the works of the flesh, but will manifest the fruit of the Spirit (22, 23). But the key to producing such fruit is "belong[ing] to Christ" (24). That life, in relationship with Jesus, is Spirit-led, and thus truly free. A life of liberty can never deteriorate to license.

Throughout chapter 6, Paul continued to discuss characteristics of the spiritually maturing Christian. First, a believer can test his spiritual maturity through restoring an erring Christian. This needs to be done gently, with the awareness that no one is immune from temptation. Next, Christians are to bear one another's burdens. Paul's language in 6:2 suggests that the burdens in question are unduly heavy, more than a person should be expected to carry. Fellow-believers should be willing to share this burden. However, in verse 5, Paul stated that each person should "bear his own load." At first reading, the sense of paradox leaps out. But a careful look at the wording resolves the problem. In contrast to the unusually heavy load of verse 2, the word Paul used for *burden* or *load* in verse 5 is quite different. Here it refers to the normal workload or responsibility that falls upon every person. Thus, verse 5 stands as a warning to anyone who might be tempted to compare himself to others and feel either smugness or self-pity. A person's fortunes, whether good or bad, should not be judged by constant comparison with others who have more or less. Thus, verse 5 is reminiscent of the incident when Peter asked the Lord what would happen to John, and Jesus replied, "Peter, your concern is to follow me, and leave John's concern with me" (see John 21:22). So verse 2 says it is fine to look around for those who need help, while verse 5 says, in effect, Don't look anywhere simply for purposes of comparison, for each of you must ultimately answer directly to God.

In his conclusion, which he penned with his own hand without the assistance of a secretary (11), Paul referred to his "large letters." Some scholars believe this implies that Paul had poor eyesight as a result of the bright light on his Damascus-road experience (Acts 9:3). Others suggest that Paul referred to inexperience in writing, or the equivalent of underscoring or italicizing. Still others suggest that he used a very robust style of writing, simply to distinguish it from the writing of his scribe. This question simply does not have a definitive answer.

While neat summaries and organizing outlines must be used with caution, one such summary outline of Galatians is helpful. Doremus Hayes suggests it in his book, *Paul and His Epistles* (Grand Rapids, Mich.: Baker, 1969), pp. 294, 295. According to Dr. Hayes, in chapters 1 and 2, Paul set forth his apostleship as initiated by God and thus independent of the authorities in Jerusalem. Hence these two chapters could be called "The Apostle of Liberty." Chapters 3 and 4 explain Paul's "Doctrine of Liberty," while chapters 5 and 6, which state the limits of freedom in Christ, might be called "The Life of Liberty." In short, the entire epistle amounts to an emancipation proclamation for all the slaves of a legal religion.

Additional readings on chapter 9

1. James Montgomery Boice, *Galatians, The Expositor's Bible Commentary*, ed. Frank E. Gaebelein (Grand Rapids, Mich.: Zondervan, 1976).

2. Ernest De Witt Burton, *Galatians: Critical and Exegetical Commentary, The International Critical Commentary*, ed. Samuel R. Driver and Charles A. Briggs (New York: Scribner's, 1928).

3. Herman N. Ridderbos, *The Epistle of Paul to the Churches of Galatia, The New International Commentary on the New Testament* (Grand Rapids, Mich.: Eerdmans, 1974).

4. Ellen G. White, *The Acts of the Apostles*, pp. 383-388.

Chapter Ten

The Human Dilemma— All Is Lost

Romans 1:1–3:20

Aside from the story in the Gospels, no single New Testament message has wielded the power and impact of Romans. The concept of righteousness by faith had wrenched Paul out of his Pharisee mind-set and confronted him with freedom in Christ. After much deliberation, he organized his thoughts on the subject, and the letter to the Romans was the result. It was after reflecting on the teachings of this letter that Martin Luther rejected the Catholic teaching on penance, and the Protestant Reformation exploded onto the scene. Later, as John Wesley listened to the reading of Luther's commentary on Romans, he felt his "heart strangely warmed," and Methodism was born. The ripple effect continues, and the passage of years has not diminished the letter's impact. From its pages shines the light of righteousness by faith that illuminates every nook and cranny of the Christian's faith structure. Without Romans, this central Christian belief could be inferred, but many important details would remain fuzzy indeed.

Its universal scope

Every other Pauline epistle was addressed to a person or group whom Paul had visited or evangelized. His letters served as follow-up instruction to his previous teaching or else as correctives of errors that had set in after he departed. In contrast, Paul addressed Romans to a group he had never visited, and thus did not deal simply with local problems of attitude or practice. Instead, it is more wide-ranging, tackling the great issues of sin and guilt and judgment and justification. To his friends and acquaintances in Corinth or Philippi, Paul sent explicit messages of correction and counsel, but to his future friends in Rome, he sent a treatise that would introduce himself and at the same time address the ageless issues of alienation and reconciliation that have haunted humans in every time and place. Accordingly, the word *all* figures largely in several passages—*all* are guilty, *all* need a Saviour, Christ died for *all*, and we are *all* one in Him.

Authorship

No serious attack has been made against the Pauline authorship of Romans. Even the liberal German scholars of the Tübingen school included Romans in the "pillar epistles" (Romans, Galatians, 1 and 2 Corinthians) that they considered unquestionably Pauline.

However, questions have been raised concerning the placement of Romans 16. This last chapter is made up primarily of greetings to nearly thirty individuals, whom Paul referred to as either co-workers or good friends. To communities he knew well, such as Corinth, where he stayed eighteen months, he sent greetings from three or four individuals, but greeted no one by name. With this in mind, the large number of personal greetings to a church he had never visited seems a bit unusual. Furthermore, the last verse of chapter 15 sounds as if Paul had concluded his epistle there—"The God of peace be with you all. Amen." Consequently, numerous scholars have concluded that the many greetings in chapter 16 somehow got detached from the letter they were meant to conclude—for example, the letter to the church in Ephesus, where Paul had lived and acquired friends for three years. But the mystery of this chapter is not without possible solutions that keep it part of the epistle to the Romans.

First, with reference to the presumed conclusion in 15:33, it was not unusual for Paul to give a brief salutation before he came to the end of a letter. Thus, in 16:20 he gave the familiar phrase, "The grace of our Lord Jesus Christ be with you," but continued to write several more verses. Similarly the phrase at the end of chapter 15 may be nothing more than a brief pause, or it may have been where Paul intended to end the letter, but he later came back to it and added chapter 16.

The more difficult issue is the content of chapter 16. The entire chapter sounds as if Paul had sent the letter to a church with which he was very familiar. He not only knew a lot of people; he seemed to know about the inner workings of the church and the prevalent attitudes of "dissensions and difficulties" (17). There were communities about which he would have known such things (e.g., Ephesus, since he lived there three years), but how would he know them about a community of Christians he had yet to visit? Furthermore, there are twenty-six specific greetings in this chapter, yet Paul usually sent only one or two general greetings when writing to churches such as Ephesus and Philippi that he knew very well. Is it really likely that he would have sent the largest number of greetings to a community he had never visited?

Possibly. Such a list of greetings to a little-known church may not be as unlikely as it seems. The only other epistle in which Paul sent such specific greetings was Colossians, and that epistle also represents a church or churches which he had not established. Perhaps he purposely avoided sending greetings to familiar churches for fear of overlooking someone, which could give rise to the accusation that he played favorites. But to an unfamiliar church, he could send a personal greeting to everyone he knew.

It is likely that many of those Paul greeted had traveled to Rome after coming into contact with him during his many travels. In those days travel was relatively unhindered, and some of those mentioned (e.g., Priscilla and Aquilla) were definitely the traveling sort. They had left Rome before and traveled to Corinth, where Paul had first met them (Acts 18:2). After following him to Ephesus, they appeared among Paul's friends who had settled in Rome (Rom. 16:3). Eight or nine years later, they were back in Ephesus (2 Tim. 4:19). While some questions of placement may remain, there is not sufficient reason to sever chapter 16 from the rest of the epistle. It is clearly Pauline in language, style, and content.

Occasion and date of the letter

Paul's third missionary journey was more of a sojourn in Ephesus than a ground-breaking missionary trip. For three years he stayed in Ephesus (Acts 20:31), establishing the church in that region. He then traveled north and west through Macedonia to Corinth, where he worked and wrote for three months (Acts 20:2, 3). While in Corinth, he solicited funds for the struggling Jerusalem church and laid plans to extend the gospel far to the west—Rome and Spain (Rom. 15:23-25). Paul's reference in Romans 16:1 to Cenchrea, a port of Corinth, and to Phoebe's imminent departure for Rome, suggests that Paul was about to send a letter to the Romans from Corinth. If that reference was made during his three-month stay in Corinth on his third missionary trip, and if the letter was, in fact, this letter to the Romans, then the date of the letter would be A.D. 56/57.

Purpose of the letter

As mentioned previously, Paul's letters are consistently reactionary—that is, they responded or reacted to conditions or problems that had been reported to him concerning a community of Christians with whom he was familiar. However, Romans is an exception to this format. It could not be reactionary in the same way as his other letters since he had never visited the area and did not have direct knowledge of the church and its situation. Inasmuch as he planned to make Rome only a stopover on his way to Spain (15:24), Paul apparently felt that his visit would be most fruitful if the members were already acquainted with his understanding of the gospel. That is why his letter to the Romans gives the most thorough and systematic presentation of his teachings to be found in all his epistles.

Theme

Since Romans was not simply a letter of response to a local problem, it is not surprising that its message has the most universal appeal of all the epistles. Humankind, burdened by many fears, feels a deep need to come into right standing with God, and this is the primary issue of the letter. The universal sinfulness of man and the universal grace of God are its central teachings. All the desperate human attempts to achieve a sense of peace and right standing with God are futile and can only generate greater and greater frustration. Furthermore, the Jew with a moral background considerably better than that of the Gentile is really no better off in this matter of acceptability with God. *All* have fallen short (3:23), but provision has been made for all by the universal gift of grace.

Organization of the letter

Although the phrase "justification by faith" is often used as a summary of the primary message of Romans, the letter covers more theological ground than that. In the first five chapters Paul worked out his teaching on justification by faith as opposed to works. Then in chapters 6-8 he changed to questions of postconversion behavior—in effect, sanctification. In chapters 9-11 Paul addressed the troubling issue of Israel's role now that Christ had come and Gentiles were as welcome in the church as Jews. Finally, in chapters 12-16, Paul focused on the postconversion Christian experience and the nature of transformed conduct, which is implied in chapters 6-8.

Paul's knowledge of the Romans

Since Paul had never visited the church at Rome, his knowledge of its members and its needs is somewhat mystifying. However, as mentioned before, travel was relatively easy and apparently commonplace. Not only had a number of Paul's friends traveled to Rome, but some had probably also brought him word of conditions in the capital city. As messages filtered in from the travelers, Paul got a relatively clear picture of the Roman believers and some of their needs.

Consequently, notwithstanding his distance from Rome, it is not surprising that his letter sounds, at times, directed to rather specific needs and circumstances.

Chapter 1—Paul's credentials and the desperate straits of the heathen

The salutation in Romans is longer than any other in Paul's epistles. One reason for its length may be that, since most of the members were unacquainted with him, he felt constrained to be more thorough than usual in his introduction. Also, though the letter contains little reproof, Paul did admonish the Roman believers here and there, and anytime a person tells another to do something, the question of authority crops up. Thus, Paul felt the need to establish his credentials, and he proceeded to do so in a methodical and impressive manner. Not only was he the servant (slave) of Christ Jesus, but he had been *called* to be an apostle, *set apart* for the gospel of God. Obviously, he wanted it understood that his mission was not his idea. His role had a divine thrust behind it.

The characteristically disjointed style of Paul's writing can be readily seen in the first seven verses. Though Paul penned these opening lines to introduce himself and his teachings, he bluntly interjected theological tidbits all along the way. For example, as soon as he mentioned the gospel, he felt that he had to explain what the word meant, so in verse 2 he took a short digression to clarify his meaning. The gospel, he said, was that which had earlier been promised through the Old Testament prophets regarding the "Son" of God. At the mention of "Son," he once again delayed the completion of his original sentence by adding, in verses 3-5, further clarification about the Son. Only in verses 6, 7 did he finally get back to the completion of the greeting he broke off after verse 1. Actually, his statements of friendship and personal concern continue all the way through verse 15. In his introduction, this style of interjecting clarifying phrases is merely interesting, but later, when his sentences carry heavier theological freight, his verbal parentheses can seem more like bumpy detours.

In chapter 1:16 Paul began his first doctrinal instruction by laying out his theme—the gospel reveals God's righteousness, and that righteousness is most clearly seen in His saving of the lost race. Or, to put it another way, the gospel is God's power to save all who believe. Paul proceeded to explain this important teaching by quoting the familiar phrase in Habakkuk 2:4, "The just shall live by faith" (KJV). However, Habakkuk clearly had in mind a sustaining faith that keeps the just person steadfast during stressful times. The idea that faith brings a person into right standing with God was simply not in Habakkuk's mind. In Habakkuk's view, the godly person already had right standing with God, and his ongoing faith keeps him from falling. Paul, on the other hand, emphasized how a person comes into right standing with God, not how he stays there. Thus, Paul gave a bit of a spin to the meaning of Habakkuk's phrase, so that whereas Habakkuk said the righteous man will *live by faith*, Paul used the phrase to say that the man who is *righteous by faith* will live.

Paul immediately explained in practical terms why the human condition makes this justifying act of God so necessary. He portrayed in graphic terms (18-32) the degenerate condition of those who have put the greatest distance between themselves and God. These verses stress both the lostness of the pagans and the inexcusableness of their condition. They were without excuse, first of all, because they had misinterpreted or rejected the evidences in the natural world that reveal the power and deity of God (19, 20). While the picture of God in nature is admittedly diffuse and *general*—not exactly a photograph—it is clear enough to confirm the guilt of those who turn away from it. In other words, natural, or general, revelation brings sufficient knowledge about God's power and greatness to indict humans for their irresponsibility, but in itself is not adequate to bring a knowledge of salvation.

At this point it is tempting to get sidetracked into a discussion of whether the revelation of God in nature is enough to bring about the saving of the heathen. But this is clearly not the issue in Romans 1. Starting with the most obvious examples, the hardhearted and impenitent heathen, Paul built his case—that all persons are not only lost but are without excuse in their lost condition. He did not attempt to deal with exceptions. He only set forth the rule—that the pagans had had sufficient knowledge to ensure their guilt. The moral degenerates described in verses 21-32 sound almost too bad to be real, but we should not underestimate the moral corruption and wickedness that characterized the large cities in Paul's day. When he wrote Romans he was living in Corinth, a city widely known for its immorality and depravity. Perhaps he was looking out his window as he penned these words of moral degeneration. The tone is indeed somber as he three times stated, "God gave them up" to the consequences of their behavior (24, 26, 28). Paul meant that phrase not merely in a permissive sense, but also in a judicial sense. In other words, it is not merely a cause-effect relationship. God's giving them up did not originate their moral condition. It was rather a divine concession to their wishes, but the outcome could only be self-aggravating. When no divine influence is brought to bear upon the human conscience, it is truly an abandonment of tragic proportions and is itself a kind of death sentence.

Chapter 2—Nice people are guilty too

Paul began chapter 2 with admonition for those who are critical of others, and quite clearly he was no longer talking about the depraved pagans. So who has suddenly come into the range of his verbal fusillade? From chapter 2:17 onward, Paul addressed the Jews explicitly. However, the object of the early verses of chapter 2 is not at once apparent. Some scholars feel that Paul's language was intentionally ambiguous so his words could refer to anyone who might feel smug in his/her moral rectitude. In this case, the language would include Jews, but would not be limited to them. Paul had just described the hopeless condition of the Gentiles and now in chapter 2 broadened the category of the hopeless to include those who feel morally superior to the Gentiles he had just described. No doubt the first group to come to mind would be the Jews, who were generally more "moral" than the societies in which they lived. But again, Paul was building his case—it's not just certain groups that are lost. The entire human race is lost, and that includes the relatively better behaved children of Abraham.

In verses 3-11 Paul differentiated between profession and practice and thereby asserted that right standing with God is equated with sincerity and penitence, not a profession of good intentions. Accordingly, when, in 2:6, he said that God will judge man "according to his works," he was not turning his back on the importance of faith. He was simply underscoring the importance of *authentic* profession as opposed to *mere* profession. The same idea is couched in different words in verse 13, where Paul asserted that it is not the "hearers of the law who are righteous before God, but the doers." In no sense does this principle conflict with Paul's teaching of justification by faith in chapters 1:17 and 3:21-25. There he dealt with how the Christian life begins. In 2:6 he referred to how life is judged at its close. At that point, sincerity of faith will be seen in the *works* of faith, not the mere *profession* of it.

Throughout chapter 2, Paul seemed to have in mind the presumptuous Jew who felt that the special relationship between God and Abraham guaranteed to Abraham's children immunity from the criteria by which others would be judged. Thus, the Jew allowed that Gentiles needed repentance, but since Jews, as descendants of Abraham, enjoyed a favored position with God, an occasional sin was not of much consequence. But Paul shocked the Jews with his assertion that before the judging eye of God, Jew and Gentile stood on the same level. In fact, the same "priority" that brought the gospel "to the Jew *first* and also to the Greek" (1:6) now applied, in 2:9, to the disasters of the day of judgment, which will also come to "the Jew first."

In verses 12-16 Paul tightened his argument against the possibility that any group of people could somehow be excusable in sin. In verse 12 he referred to two categories of people—those who sinned "without the law" (probably Gentiles) and those who sinned "under the law" (probably Jews). The suggestion in verse 14 that some Gentiles inadvertently do the right thing and thus are "a law to themselves" often brings up the issue of the necessity and content of Christian evangelism. If some kind of spiritual intuition can actually bring a person into a saving relationship with God, what is the role of the gospel commission? But such a question was far from Paul's argument. In this passage Paul had in mind the equity and fairness of God's condemning judgment, not how certain Gentiles can have sufficient knowledge to be saved apart from the law. Paul made no suggestion that any who are without the law actually gain eternal life. He was simply establishing solidly that *no salvation* for any person is based on works. Thus, both Jew and Gentile had sinned, and both had done so against the law. While Gentiles had no Decalogue, they did have the moral guide of conscience, which rendered them guilty. Accordingly, the Jew was the more guilty since he had not only conscience (even the Gentile had that), but also the written law to condemn him. Thus, Paul's main point was that both Jew and Gentile stood guilty before God. The Jew could not claim exemption because he did not have the law; he would be judged as one who had the law but went against it. The clear emphasis of the passage is upon who is lost and why. It is not upon who might be saved.

In the remainder of chapter 2 Paul expounded on two elements of Judaism that illustrate ways the Jews had fallen short of the divine expectation. First, there was the matter of the Jewish attitude toward their possession of the law—that this made them superior to the Gentiles. But not only did the Gentiles already have a law, Paul said (14), but the Jews had not consistently kept theirs (21, 22), and their inconsistencies had brought disrepute upon the name of God among the Gentiles (24).

Similarly, the Jews had raised circumcision to a position of undue importance, as something isolated from moral behavior. Paul tried to lessen the emphasis they put on the rite and showed that circumcision and law keeping are inextricably linked. While circumcision is the symbol of Judaism, law keeping is the substance, and the symbol without the substance is of little value. In fact, in the true valuation of things, the Gentile who kept the law but was uncircumcised ranked higher than the Jew who was circumcised but failed in his observance of law. In verse 25 Paul said that the symbol had value, but only when there was a clear connection between symbol and substance, circumcision and law keeping.

Chapter 3:1-20—There is no recourse, all is lost

In view of what had gone before, the question with which Paul began chapter 3 is a logical one: If the law-keeping Gentile was better off than the law-breaking Jew, what was the advantage of the Jew? Wouldn't such a concept nullify the entire meaning of the rich Jewish heritage? His answer— "Much . . . to begin with" (2)—implies the beginning of a list of advantages. The problem is, Paul broke the list off after the first item and did not continue it until 9:4, 5. This longest sidetrack in the New Testament is typical of Paul. He started his list of advantages by referring to the privilege the Jews had in possessing the "oracles," or words, of God, particularly the covenant promises. But when he mentioned the broken covenant, he was immediately diverted from his list of "advantages" to pursue the notion that somehow God had not kept His word. Even though the faithlessness was on the part of some Jews, didn't the broken covenant somehow implicate God? Paul dismissed this charge with the emphatic assertion that God would still be true even if every man were false.

But in verses 5, 7 he addressed a related objection. If human wrong serves to highlight and demonstrate God's goodness, should not the human guilt be lessened or even dismissed? In answer, Paul continued his logic by agreeing that in such case it would be difficult for God to "judge" the world. But then he quickly reversed his line of reasoning and said that since we know God is going to judge the world, humans must be guilty.

At first reading, the implication of verse 9 that Jews were no better off than Gentiles seems to fly in the face of the statement in 3:2 that they had advantages. But verses 1, 2 refer to the distinctive opportunities of the Jews in God's overall plan, whereas verse 9 refers to the Jews' spiritual fitness before God. In this latter respect, the Jew had no edge over the Gentile—both stood under the power and condemnation of sin. The OT quotations that run from verses 10-18 simply underscore the hopelessness of the spiritual condition of both Jew and Gentile.

Paul's sweeping indictment of the race, which began in 1:18, comes to a climax in 3:19, 20. His first use of "law" in verse 19 no doubt refers to the Old Testament in general, and his reference to those "under the law" probably means Jews in particular. But by his phrase "so that every mouth may be stopped," he showed that if Jews are guilty, then the entire race is lost. In other words, if those who had the best chance are lost, then there is no question about the fate of all the others. This sweeping condemnation of the race and the law as the vehicle of that guilt all comes together in verses 19, 20. Whatever else the law does, it reveals sin, but in no way does it ameliorate sin's results. Every person stands hopelessly condemned before God's bar of judgment. The scorching argument that Paul began in 1:18 comes to its depressing conclusion in 3:20. But hope springs to life in 3:21.

Additional readings on chapter 10

1. Paul Achtemeier, *Romans*, Interpretation: A Bible Commentary for Teaching and Preaching Series (Atlanta: John Knox Press, 1985).
2. William Barclay, *The Letter to the Romans*, The Daily Study Bible (Philadelphia: Westminster, 1975).
3. C. K. Barrett, *The Epistle to the Romans, Harper's New Testament Commentaries* (New York, Evanston, Ill., and London: Harper and Row, 1958).
4. James D. G. Dunn, *Romans 1-8, Word Biblical Commentary* (Dallas: Word, 1988).
5. Everett F. Harrison, *Romans*, vol. 10 of *The Expositor's Bible Commentary*, ed. Frank E. Gaebelein (Grand Rapids, Mich.: Zondervan, 1978).
6. John Murray, *The Epistle to the Romans, The New International Commentary on the New Testament* (Grand Rapids, Mich.: Eerdmans, 1971).
7. William Sanday and Arthur Headlam, *Romans: A Critical and Exegetical Commentary, The International Critical Commentary*, ed. Samuel R. Drivers and Alfred Plummer (Edinburgh: T. and T. Clark, 1911).
8. Ellen G. White, *The Acts of the Apostles*, pp. 372-382.

Eleven

The Divine Solution

Romans 3:21–5:21

Chapter 3:21-31—The gospel summarized

Having brought the human condition to the depths of hopelessness in 3:20, Paul now lifted the gaze of lost humans to the source of life and hope. He introduced the new order of things with a strong contrast—"but now." Righteousness, he said, comes from God and embraces humanity, not because the race is deserving, but because it is helpless. And so God's solution is offered for man's dilemma. Some scholars feel that the six verses in 3:21-26 comprise the high point of Paul's reasoning on justification and the focal point of the entire epistle to the Romans. Luther put a mark opposite verse 25 and wrote in the margin, "Mark this; this is the chief point and the very central place of the epistle and of the whole Bible" (Doremus Hayes, *Paul and His Epistles* [Grand Rapids, Mich.: Baker, 1969], p. 318).

Any discussion of righteousness by faith must, at some point, clearly define the term *righteousness*. Throughout Romans, when Paul referred to the righteousness of God, he consistently meant God's act of saving lost humans. Such is clearly seen in the wording of 3:26, where Paul made a play on the word and said, in effect, that God is "righteous, and the one who makes righteous."

However, when the term *righteous* or *righteousness* is attributed to humans, Paul generally had one of two meanings in mind. First, there is the forensic, legal sense, in which a person is declared to be righteous apart from any consideration of merit or moral right-doing. This legal declaration that proclaims guilty persons innocent is the sense which predominates in Paul's writings and is the only sense in Romans 1-5. The second definition of righteousness is a moral righteousness, which includes elements of right-doing. Paul discussed this definition in connection with the topic of sanctification, which comes into focus in Romans 8 and 12.

With regard to the definition of forensic righteousness, whereby God pronounces guilty humans innocent, the conclusion might be drawn that God is involved in a kind of legal fiction. How can sinners be called innocent and God not be called a liar? In answer, while the verdict of acquittal is for all sinners, not every sinner will ultimately be pronounced righteous. Obviously, hard-core rebellious people who are impenitent to the end cannot be called righteous in spite of their rebellion. To be effective, any legal decision must be received and acted upon, and when that happens, the sinner is a very different person.

While this responsive attitude does not equal moral perfection, it does indicate that now something is different about the sinner. He or she is not the same person as before. Even if his position hasn't changed much, the direction of his life has changed, and that makes a great deal of difference. Before repentance, the sinner was oriented toward self and the world. Now, his face is toward God. Because of this change of direction he is indeed righteous, not in the quantitative sense of being morally perfect, but in a qualitative, potential sense. The person has not suddenly, overnight, become a perfect ten on some scale of morality. Instead, the person has now willingly inscribed his or her name on the scale.

To proclaim such a person righteous simply acknowledges that his status has now changed, and that involves no legal fiction. Keep in mind, God has taken the initiative, and the sinner has simply *responded* to the divine initiative. Accordingly, the response carries with it no merit in itself—it is simply the spirit of trust and acceptance, which God then reckons as righteousness. Paul summed it up neatly in verses 24, 25: People are justified by grace as a gift through the redemption worked out through Jesus, and faith is the human response that reaches out to receive what God offers in Christ. Therefore, we should always describe it as right-eousness *by grace, through faith.*

In chapter 3:25, that cumbersome word often translated *propitiation* begs for definition. The RSV renders it "expia-tion," but that is little help, as neither word is part of the everyday vocabulary of twentieth-century people, though it was widely known and used in Paul's day. Unfortunately, its predominate sense in society outside of the Christian circles was that of appeasing or placating, perhaps even bribing an angry, unpredictable god. This meaning is thoroughly con-sistent in its nonbiblical usage. Furthermore, it is used in the New Testament only here and in a slightly different form in 1 John 2:2 and 4:10. Such limited usage makes it difficult to cross-check for additional meaning and insight.

It appears, however, that Paul intentionally used the word to drive home a point. He must have known how the word would sound, and so he used it to teach both pagans and Christians something important about Christian theology. Given the historical context, Paul's usage strongly suggests that there is something like anger in the Christian's God. In fact, without this element, the word would be quite meaning-less. Of course, to pagans, there was nothing surprising or unacceptable about the idea of an angry god—all their gods got angry. But such an idea is not so amenable to Christians. We find it difficult to think of our God as angry or wrathful. Yet rejecting all aspects of God's anger is a misunderstand-ing of both God's holiness and the consequences of sin.

A stoic, unimpassioned God, totally unmoved by human actions and reactions, is simply not the biblical picture of God. Rather, God leaps from the inspired page as One who is constantly active in the affairs of humans, rejoicing in their joys and grieving at their rebellion and suffering. In fact, the Old Testament makes no apologies for the numerous de-scriptions of His anger against the gross depravity of men and women. And while the New Testament spells out the nature of His incredible mercy in His Son, it speaks in no uncertain terms of His wrath against sin (1:18). Apparently something in God's character recoils against sin, and that reaction can only be described in terms of very strong aversion, such as anger or hatred. Furthermore, to work out a plan of atonement whereby sinful man and holy God might be reconciled, it was necessary to deal with that aspect of God's character.

Bearing all this in mind, Paul unabashedly used the pagan term *expiation* but gave the word a radical new twist. In the Christian scheme of things, sin is so serious that God simply cannot look the other way, nor can He be bought off by some pathetic offering thrown up to Him by a frantic worshiper. Instead, Paul spun the heads of his pagan listeners by asserting that God provides for the expiation of His own anger. Unheard of! Satisfying the demands of a capricious god—that they could understand, but not like this! So while the Christian message is similar to the pagan insofar as the need to meet the demands of God, it is very different in that God Himself offers the means of reconciliation. Fearful man is not left to grope about for some mystical offering to appease the anger of his unpredictable god. The anger of the Christian God is as real as the means of turning that anger. God's own Son experienced it ("My God . . . why hast thou forsaken me?"), offered what was required, and now extends to all believers the benefit of His victory. "There is . . . now no condemnation for those who are in Christ Jesus" (8:1). So the message of the cross is truly unique, for at this one point, anger and forgiveness, justice and mercy, meet. And the resultant reconciliation of man and God is then passed on to all who will acknowledge, by means of a trusting faith, that it has been done for them. Through it all, the sacrifice of Christ is not made to persuade the Father to once again love and trust His wayward children. The sacrifice is made solely *because* the Father loved His wayward children. As Paul says in chapter 5:6, "While we were still helpless . . . Christ died for the ungodly" (NASB). Once again Paul's expression in 3:26 comes to mind—God is both "righteous and the one who makes righteous."

In 3:27-31 Paul stressed again that this process of justification is solely by faith, so the Jew had no advantage over the Gentile. But for many of his hearers, such an assertion immediately raised the ugly specter of antinomianism—no-law-ism. But Paul anticipated the charge and denied it categorically in verse 31. He did not go on to give his reasons for such a cavalier dismissal of the accusation; this he would do in chapter 6. It was enough here to show that he was aware of the implications of his position and thereby served notice to his enemies that they should suspend their objections.

Chapter 4—Old Testament
illustrations of righteousness by faith

In the Jewish view of things, Abraham was the flawless father figure upon whom rested their entire structure of acceptability with God. Paul, fully aware of this, reasoned that if he could show that Abraham's case actually spoke in favor of the faith argument, his position would be immeasurably strengthened, and the Jewish stress on merit righteousness would fall to the ground. Paul approached the problem by talking about the advantage of the Jew and the attitude of boasting. Since Abraham was richly rewarded, he might have had something to boast about—but only if he had some merit to present. Paul made it clear that Abraham's faith was "*reckoned to him* as righteousness," so obviously his faith was not meritorious in itself, and thus Abraham, the great, exemplary patriarch, had nothing of his own about which he could boast.

Paul next referred to David, that other great hero of Old Testament Judaism, to show that his case, like that of Abraham, spoke in favor of the Christian position on faith. Here Paul alluded to Psalm 32:1, 2, where David embodied Paul's very argument, only in a negative way. If through the experience of forgiveness a man's sins are *not reckoned* against him, apparently he is being treated better than he deserves, and this is another way of describing grace in action. So Paul showed that both great patriarchs, Abraham and David, supported his view of righteousness by grace through faith.

To further illustrate his point, Paul reminded his Jewish listeners (9-12) that even the circumcision of Abraham spoke in favor of God's grace, since it took place *after* God reckoned him righteous. Therefore, it could not be his Jewishness or his circumcision that made him somehow acceptable to God. Rather, his circumcision was a sign or seal of something that preceded it. It was not a meaningless rite, but neither was it of value in and of itself. It was of value only as it set the seal on a previous experience of genuine faith. Without that antecedent faith, the rite was empty of meaning.

This had obvious implications for Gentiles, who, in a sense, were waiting in the wings. Thus, when Paul asserted in verse 16 that the promise to Abraham was to *all* his descendants who shared his faith, not just to the adherents of the law, the message for Gentile believers was apparent. Abraham was not the father of circumcised believers only. He was the father of many nations (18), since his faith set him apart, and there are people with faith like his in many nations.

It is easy for people to agree that Abraham was a great man of faith. What is not so clear is the connection between his good behavior and God's promises of offspring like the sand of the sea. In Romans 4:13-15 Paul addressed that issue by asserting that God gave the promise to Abraham because of his faith, not because he was a good law keeper. In fact, the function of law is to bring condemnation, not righteousness. In verse 15 Paul put it very tersely—"The law brings wrath." His thought here seems to be: Humans are sinners (law breakers), and as such they must die, since that is the consequence of sin (6:23). Since the unmet demand of the law causes our condemnation and death, in a way, the law can be spoken of as that which brings upon us the wrath of God. But Paul condensed all this into "the law brings wrath," thereby neatly jumping over all the intermediate explanation that man's *transgression of the law* brings about the wrath.

Throughout chapter 4 Paul underscored in various ways that faith kept Abraham linked to God through all his difficult times. But he never spoke of Abraham's faith as a good work, but rather as that which was *reckoned* to him as righteousness. It is interesting to note that in verses 24, 25 Paul equated the Christian's belief in Christ's resurrection with Abraham's belief that God could produce a son through his and Sarah's worn-out bodies. He offered such belief as a fitting illustration of that trusting relationship which is reckoned as righteousness.

Chapter 5—The rich rewards of the reconciled

Paul now directed attention to some of the immediate rewards of being justified by faith, and they are rich indeed. First, there is peace. While the most ancient texts support the sense of exhortation in verse 1 ("let us have peace,"), the statement of fact ("we have peace") fits Paul's thought more naturally and is the choice of most present-day scholars. Since we now stand justified before God, peace of mind is a given. But there is more. Now there is rejoicing in the hope of the glory to come, and through the Holy Spirit there is a fuller awareness of the depth of God's love.

The demonstration of that love is so impressive that Paul sounds in verses 6-8 as if he could scarcely believe it, let alone describe it. Christ's loving sacrifice was made for a totally unappreciative, unlovely, unattractive people. This is so contrary to our way of thinking that a human analogy is difficult to imagine. Clearly, the death of Christ did not cause God to love sinful humans. It is evidence that He already loved us. It is love that caused the sacrifice, not the other way around. Humans tend to love those who are already good or "righteous" or in some small way, deserving. But even in that setting, the ultimate sacrifice, the giving of one's life for another, is almost unheard of. But God's self-sacrificing love is not based on anything favorable in the recipients. "While we were still helpless [Greek, "sick"] . . . while we were yet sinners" (NASB), Paul cried, Christ died for us. So it was not for deserving, lovely, responsive people that Christ sacrificed so much. It was for wretched, uncaring enemies that He came and gave all.

Paul built his reasoning with the a fortiori argument in verse 10. If, while we were in a state of alienation, Christ sacrificed all for us, how much more, now that we are in a state of reconciliation, will God see to it that, by the resurrected life of Christ, we will be saved to the uttermost (11). In other words, if enemies can be reconciled, how much more certain is it that friends can live together forever?

In the last half of chapter 5, Paul described an Adam humanity and a Christ humanity that present some striking comparisons and contrasts. Verse 12 traces to its source the predicament Paul so graphically described in the first three chapters—the sin that brought death to the entire race began with Adam. Clear enough. But Paul never could seem to get far without raising questions that require complex answers. For example, when he stated that the universality of the death sentence is "because [or "in whom"] all men sinned," what kind of sinning is this? Some scholars suggest that the aorist tense Paul used at the end of verse 12 ("all men *sinned*") implies that the sinning referred to was at one point in time and therefore refers to Adam's sin in Eden, in which all his posterity participated vicariously. So, then, Adam's sin that spread to all was, like his death, something that spread to all. It was inherited from the father of the race. Thus, according to the Oriental idea of solidarity, the head of a race and the members of that race are all directly connected, so that the members participate in all the decisive actions of the head.

Paul seems to be drawing on that notion by what he added in verses 13, 14. Prior to Sinai, there was no law, and since it is necessary to have a law to have sin (5:13; 7:7), there should have been no sin during this period. But since "death reigned from Adam to Moses," some kind of sin must have been present to cause death. Whatever the sin was, it was "not like the transgression of Adam" (14). The usual interpretation is that the sin and death which existed from Adam to Moses was a direct consequence of Adam's sin on all his descendants. Not every person was guilty because of personal acts of sin just like Adam's. That is precisely what their sins were not—like Adam's. Theirs was an inherited guilt— they could not be born untainted and still be related to Adam. And while all his offspring down to the time of Moses committed acts of rebellion somewhat like those of Adam, none of them started with the untainted nature of Adam and then sinned against an express command of God. So in the sense that his was a *representative act* which involved many others, he was a "type of the one who was to come" (14).

In verses 15-19 Paul drew a series of parallels and contrasts between the acts of the two "Adams," with emphasis on the contrasts. Repeatedly he used the a fortiori argument to show the vast superiority of the act of the "one man Jesus Christ." In almost every verse from 15-20, the wording "how much more" is either stated or implied. Thus, while Adam and Christ were similar in that each spoke or acted as a representative of the many, they are as much different as grace is superior to the trespass. Paul made it clear that the free gift not only cancels the effects of Adam's sin in order to bring man back to innocence, but it goes so far as to offer the race *more* than it had before sin, for the gift includes righteousness (17), which leads to eternal life (21).

In verses 20, 21 Paul referred to law just as he had already done in 3:20 and did again in 7:8-12. He could not deal adequately with the great issues of sin and righteousness without considering the function of the law. Here he didn't elaborate, though. He merely used law as a foil to again point up the incredibly superior nature of grace. Not until people see the seriousness of their trespass (which the law points out) can they appreciate the superabundance of God's grace. So Paul reminded the Romans in verse 20 that, with the introduction of the law, guilt and sin become more specific and focused. To rebel against a known command is always more serious than to merely fall short of an ideal. And so in a sense, the giving of the law can be spoken of as increasing the trespass. But the "bottom line" in verse 21 is that, while sin reigns in death, grace is even more powerful—it reigns through righteousness to eternal life through Jesus Christ.

Additional readings on chapter 11

Supplementary reading can be done from the sources listed at the end of chapter 10.

Chapter
Twelve

The Meaning of
Freedom From Sin

Romans 6-8

When a person is baptized into Christ, an exhilarating sense of freedom and cleanness often results. It is truly a liberating experience when a person is reconciled with God. In Romans 3-5 Paul attempted to describe various elements of that reconciliation, which is now available in the free gift of Jesus Christ. But the act of faith that culminates in baptism is normally followed by a life of faith in which the joy and confidence are diminished by fears and uncertainty. Paul now turns to this postbaptismal experience in Romans 6-8. Apparently a number of believers were unclear about the way in which baptism united them to Christ and also about what the "in-Christ life" really meant.

Chapter 6—The meaning of Christian baptism

In chapter 3:31 Paul acknowledged that his line of reasoning to that point pushed his hearers directly toward antinomianism ("Does faith abolish law?"), but he summarily dismissed the charge ("By no means!"), while giving no explanation. Now, in 6:1, he raised essentially the same question in a slightly different form ("Can a Christian continue in sin after his conversion?"), and this time he proceeded to answer it in a systematic manner.

The first reason Paul gave for not continuing in sin after conversion is that reconciliation involves a death to sin, so any continuation of a life of sin is a logical impossibility. Furthermore, the way Paul used the term *baptism* is itself a kind of death experience. (While the paramount issue of verses 3, 4 is union with Christ, not the *mode* of baptism, clearly the method of baptism that most clearly matches the symbols of death, burial, and resurrection is baptism by immersion.)

Paul's use of the baptism figure for the Christian's union with Christ makes clear that he spoke of an objective reality, not merely a mystical feeling. A real event has taken place. The believer is a different person because of his baptism. As mentioned previously with reference to 5:12, according to the Oriental notion of solidarity, the head of a race and his descendants are linked, so that the descendants participate in all the important decisions of the head. And, just as we participated vicariously in the decisive acts of Adam, the physical head of our race, so now, by the link of baptism, we participate in the decisive acts of our spiritual head, Christ, and the most decisive acts of all are His death and resurrection.

But the figures of spiritual death and resurrection pose problems. Being baptized into the death of Christ (4) parallels the crucifixion of the "old man" (6, KJV), and walking in a new life (4) parallels being free from sin (6, 7). The problem is this: To what extent is the ensuing life really free from sin? Does the death of the "old man" result in total sinlessness thereafter?

Bear in mind that Paul often looked upon sin, not as a series of moral lapses, but as a power in the life, under whose bondage the sinner lives. Accordingly, to be free from sin is to have sin "cast down from its throne" (Anders Nygren, *Commentary on Romans* [Philadelphia: Muhlenberg Press, 1949], p. 242). Sin as a power is now defeated. Yet verse 6 is divided with the little phrase *so "that* the body of sin might be destroyed" (KJV). In other words, the death of the old man and the annulling of the body of sin are not exactly synonymous. The first makes the second possible. In other words, the death of the "old man" is the necessary beginning of a process that can result in total victory, but it is not the total victory by itself.

This interpretation helps to explain Paul's exhortations in verses 12, 13. At first reading it sounds strange that, after describing the death of the "old man" of sin, Paul should counsel the Christian to "let not sin . . . reign in your mortal bodies." It seems like such unnecessary counsel after he had just stated that the Christian has died to sin once and for all (10). However, when we think of sin as a power that has been defeated it is possible to say, "Therefore, don't let it lord it over you." Prior to the believer's "baptism into His death," such admonition would have been ludicrous. But now, since the "old man" is dead, the Christian should not live as if he is still alive. In other words, "Be what you are!"

At this point, the admonition in verse 11 is especially pertinent. For even though decisive events have taken place in the believer's life, unless he continually *reckons* himself as alive to God and dead to sin, the effect will be lost. So, while the concrete event of baptism has happened, "it rests with [the individual believer] to recognize this fact in a deliberate reorientation of his own mind. Unless he '*considers* himself dead to sin,' he is in effect not dead to sin. . . . The steady intention of mind and will is needed to make explicit in fact what is already given in principle" (C. H. Dodd, *The Epistles of Paul to the Romans* [London: Hodder and Stoughton, 1954], p. 93, emphasis supplied).

The person who *realizes* his new status, who *meditates* upon his new potential, will not be content to go on living under the tyranny of law. Paul felt so certain of this change that in verse 14 he used the future tense: "Sin *will not* lord it over you" now that you have been set free from the "under law" experience. Such an assertion does not annul the importance of the Decalogue as an objective guide for Christians, but it does do away with the condemning aspects of the law. In 6:14 Paul seems to have had in mind that aspect of law that causes sin to increase (5:20), that condemns its subjects and brings them under a kind of slavery. Whatever view of law Paul was presenting in 6:14, it could not go counter to his leadoff question in 6:1, which he repeated in 6:15. Grace means freedom, but not freedom to sin. Freedom from law means freedom from the condemnation of the law, but this does not mean the believer is free to tear loose in reckless abandon. Because grace is now present, the believer is truly free to live a sober, upright, godly live (Titus 2:11, 12).

Apparently the charge of antinomianism or libertinism was a stubborn one, and Paul tried vigorously to put it to rest. Thus the issue of both verses 1 and 15 is the same— continuance in sin. In the first fourteen verses of the chapter, Paul used the figure of our death in Christ to deny any possibility of continuing to live in sin. Then, in verses 15-23, he looked at the same question, but denied it with a metaphor from slavery. Thus, just as a slave can be under obligation to only one master at a time and is "free" of any obligation to anyone else, so it is with slaves of Jesus. Obedience to Him rules out obedience to any other master. So then, in answer to the question in verse 15 about continuance in sin, verse 16 says, Once you have chosen your master, you have committed yourself to obey. Thus, willful persistence in sin, which is a kind of loyalty to another master, is inconceivable. So the question raised in 6:1, 15 Paul answered decisively: The experience of faith starts a new life with a new master. To continue in sin after that is to attempt to bring back the old life or swear loyalty to two masters—a totally ludicrous idea.

But Paul's metaphor of slavery has an unusual element— this slave is free to choose his master, and that choice carries weighty implications. To these consequences, Paul next turned in verses 20-23. On the one hand, enslavement to sin results in moral deterioration and death, while enslavement to God results in sanctification and eternal life. But the term *sanctification* has given rise to considerable discussion. The following diagram helps to partially explain the meaning of this important word *sanctification*.

Point 1 illustrates the time when a person says Yes to the impressions of the Holy Spirit, accepts the Lord as his or her Saviour, and is reconciled to God. We often speak of this experience as *justification*. The vertical line from 1 to 2 is not a process, but rather the change of position effected by God's declaration of righteousness on behalf of the sinner. The sinner's standing before God—his *status*—is now perfect and complete because Christ's righteousness has been made his

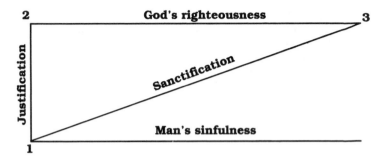

(Diagram taken from Everett F. Harrison, *Romans*, vol. 10 of *The Expositor's Bible Commentary*, ed. Frank E. Gaebelein [Grand Rapids, Mich.: Zondervan, 1976], p. 67.)

righteousness. Since he is now in Christ, his *status* with God is all it should be. In fact, it couldn't be better and will never be better. Forty more years of living the Christian life will not make this believer more acceptable with God.

But God is concerned, not just for the believer's status, but also for his or her *state*. At the time a person is justified he begins a process of growth that we sometimes call sanctification, and that is represented by the diagonal line between 1 and 3. So then justification is a change of status that starts a process called sanctification, which will result in the person's actual state growing gradually toward his or her status. The much-argued point about when a person's *status* and *state* become identical (perfectionism) is irrelevant in the present passage. It is sufficient to know that justification frees us from the clutches of sin and death and brings sanctification and eternal life, all of which are the result of simply choosing to be a slave of God.

Chapter 7—Jurisdiction of law

Paul didn't quite finish his "death in Christ" metaphor in chapter 6. So in 7:1-6 he mined it for one more application. Here he reminded the believers that law has jurisdiction over a person only as long as he lives, and since the believer has "died" in Christ's death, he is released from any power the law may have exercised over him prior to his "death." The connection is made very clear in 7:4: "You have died to the law through the body of Christ, so that you may belong to another."

But such an argument only raises the larger question of the law's function. In the last part of chapter 6 and the first part of chapter 7, Paul seems to have used the phrases "free from sin" and "free from law" as if they were synonymous. Yet sin and law are not identical, though they do have a kind of working relationship. In 7:7, the function of the law is restated in terms similar to those in 3:20—it makes sin known. But in verse 13 Paul added that, when sin can work through the agency of law, it becomes "sinful beyond measure." Still, while Paul spoke of the law "increas[ing] the trespass" (5:20), he did not say that the law created sin. Rather, in verses 8, 9 he asserted that before the law, sin lay dormant, but it was there. So then the law was not the originator of sin. It was merely the vehicle through which sin could come alive and do its work.

Sin could only do this, not through some inherent weakness in the law, but through the weakness of the flesh (8:3). In fact, Paul hastened to exonerate the law by his acclamation in verse 12 that "the law is holy . . . and just and good." He could assert this only by repeatedly pointing out that the perversity is in the flesh, not the law. Sin and the flesh can be spoken of as evil, but not the law. Even though the law plays a role in condemnation, Paul still spoke of it as "good" in verse 13. In fact, the one element of unity that runs throughout chapter 7 is exoneration of the law. Thus it is not accidental that after his negative-sounding analogy in verses 1-6 Paul spent so much time stressing that the weakness is not in the law but in the human.

But he must now explain how something so good can bring about death (13). The answer is that Paul looked upon sin as a sinister power that uses the weakness of the flesh and the condemning aspect of the law to defeat people. But, as in chapters 1-3, he again made humans appear hopeless for the sole purpose of offering them hope for their hopelessness.

But the hopelessness needs to be more vivid, so in verses 14-24 Paul gave it a face. Over the years, considerable debate has raged over both the time of the experience and the identity of the "I" in these verses. Is Paul here describing his own experience, and if so, which experience? Is this a description of his tortured pre-Christian life as a Pharisee or of a frustrated, largely unsuccessful attempt to live the Christian life? The most popular view is the latter, but it does pose some problems.

The problem

If chapter 7:14-24 describes the frustrations of Paul's life as a Christian, then what about the picture of victory painted in 6:6-11? Both passages cannot exist in the same person at the same time. It is simply not reasonable to insist that a man can crucify his old self, no longer be enslaved to sin, be freed from sin, and then go on to say that he is carnal, sold under sin, doing the things he knows are wrong. Furthermore, it is not adequate to say that Paul merely described in chapter 7 the tensions inherent in living the Christian life amidst the usual temptations. What he described is not an occasional disappointment but an experience of *total frustration* in which the person goes on being a "captive to the law of sin" (23).

The pre-Christian, ideal-man hypothesis

The best solution to the "who" and "when" of verses 14-24 is a somewhat complicated one. It is possible that Paul used a rhetorical "I" in this section, combining elements of his own experience and the experiences of others to create a kind of ideal person. On this basis, his use of the first-person pronoun throughout these verses would be like an editorial "we." It is not unknown for Paul to use such a rhetorical approach. In 2 Corinthians 12:2 he used this approach to describe a real experience as though it were rhetorical ("I know a man in Christ . . ."). But in Romans 7 he reversed the technique. He described an experience that was at least partially rhetorical as if it were real. Thus verses 14-24 describe an experience of frustration and defeat that may have been a part of his earlier life (at least it is typical of unconverted people everywhere), but it could be seen and described in these terms only by a converted Christian.

Before he had come to Christ, he would not have spoken this way, and, in fact, could not have accurately described his former experience at all. Such expressions as those found in verses 18, 22, 25 would be totally incongruous in the mouth of an unconverted person. Saying that they refer to an unregenerate experience does not mean that the one describing the experience is at the moment of expression, still unconverted. Not until grace had come upon him could Paul have had the view he presented here.

So as the converted Paul reflected, he remembered clearly that earlier experience of defeat, so common among the unconverted Jews, but now he perceived its true meaning and used the appropriate terms. So the experience he described was past, but the words he used to describe it came from his present stance and vocabulary, which were Christian. Thus Paul was saying something like, "Now that I am a Christian, I can see that the problem with all of us is the carnal, selfish 'I.' In fact, the selfishness is so all-consuming that Paul saw it as a "body of death" (24). But then comes the joyous solution: "Thanks be to God through Jesus Christ our Lord!" This beautiful experience of liberation and deliverance is so graphically described in verse 25 that the sense of contrast with the preceding verses also argues for the view that verses 14-24 are preconversion, and verse 25a *introduces* the incredible solution.

But then there is 25b, which seems to take away the exhilaration of both 25a and the great freedom of 8:1, 2. Right in the middle of giving thanks to God that through Christ he was no longer condemned, Paul inserted the sobering thought that his mind served the law of God, but his flesh served the law of sin. The problem can be handled in a couple of ways. The solution most in keeping with the foregoing interpretation looks upon 25b as a summarizing flashback to the former experience that Paul had just described. Having broken in with the great deliverance from the body of death, he took another moment to remember that without Christ it was a pitched battle between his mind's knowing the law and his flesh doing otherwise.

Another view is that 25b is an admission that even after

Christ comes in, I may attempt to serve God "by myself," the effort will be doomed, and I will only end up serving the law of sin.

Chapter 8—Freedom and walking by the Spirit

The way Paul kept referring to the law, it is easy to conclude that many of his first listeners were quite preoccupied with law keeping. In chapters 5-7 he accentuated various limitations of the law, but, in 7:25–8:2, he brought into dramatic focus the sense of futility and the sense of relief experienced by the person who has felt the full impact of law domination and has been set free in Christ. In the preceding chapters he had referred to several kinds of freedom—from wrath (chapter 5), from sin (chapter 6), and from law (chapter 7). In 8:2-4 Paul referred to perhaps the greatest freedom—freedom from death. That freedom was purchased by the "law of the Spirit of life in Christ Jesus" (2). But what is the Spirit of life in Christ Jesus?

His explanation in verses 3, 4 helps to clarify how this freedom comes into the human experience. First, he showed that the law is incapable of bringing freedom, not because it has inherent flaws, but because the humans trying to keep it are all flawed. Keeping this in mind is a necessary prelude to understanding what God did; that is, He sent His own Son in the "likeness of sinful flesh," and in that "likeness" Christ defeated sin. Sin could only touch Christ in His human nature, so when He died victoriously on the cross in that nature, He broke the power of sin over that nature. Thereafter, sin could bring no charge against Him. More than that, sin would now be powerless against the believer who "died with Christ." Once and for all, sin was condemned in the flesh of Christ.

For all of Paul's discussion of justification and dying with Christ, it is surprising that, up to this point, the role of the Holy Spirit has not been exactly prominent. Chapter 6 contains no mention of the Spirit, and chapters 5 and 7 make only one reference each. But in chapter 8 there is a notable change. Paul implied that the life of the justified believer is to be a life lived in the Spirit. In the process, he referred to the Spirit nineteen times in this one chapter. As is common with Paul, his use of the term for *Spirit* takes several turns throughout the chapter, but his predominant meaning seems to be the empowering influence that works out within us the pleasing of God. This power brings about peace and life (6) and is synonymous with "Christ . . . in you" (10). Furthermore, Christ, by His Spirit, does not merely give us the power to fulfill the demand of righteousness. It is not that He gives me the strength, and I do the work. Verse 3 must be kept before us: "God has done . . ." What is worked out in the Christian's life is the fruit of the Spirit, not the fruit of the Christian.

At the same time, although the Spirit fulfills the requirement of the law "in us" (4), our continuing Christian experience is affected by how we use our minds. The text literally says that those who "are" according to the flesh put their mind on the things of flesh, and the same is true for those of the Spirit. So, while Christians "are" of the Spirit, there must also be a following and a yielding to Him that begins in the mind. Victorious Christians, then, can be described as those persons whose minds are daily turned toward the Spirit, and who, by that Spirit which "dwells in you" (9), are then empowered to be "sons [and daughters] of God" (14).

Harassment and persecution of Roman Christians had bedeviled the church for several years by the time Paul wrote to them, so beginning in verse 18, the apostle turned to the subject of encouragement for truly trying times. The first basis of encouragement he offered is the extent to which the future glory will outweigh the present difficulties. In effect, he said that there is no comparison, since the future glory so far exceeds the present suffering. In fact, through his use of personification, Paul made creation itself cry out in eager anticipation for the glorious time of renewal that is soon to come.

The second basis for encouraging the suffering saints is the constant intercession and guidance of the Spirit (26, 27). Whatever human weakness he has, the struggling Christian can be assured that the Spirit understands the deepest human longings and works in close cooperation with the Father for our salvation. Hence, the Christian can be encouraged that although he often feels great emotional and physical distance from God, the Spirit of God is at his elbow and fully understands his every inarticulate mumbling. Furthermore, since the Spirit stays in constant touch with God, the Christian can be assured that God knows exactly when and how much he suffers and will be there to encourage and sustain.

The third basis for encouragement lies in the consolation and assurance that, for believers, God is at work in all the varied happenings of life (28-30). Contrary to some popular interpretations, the text does not mean that whatever comes must have a divine origin or purpose. Many of the events and circumstances that flood the Christian's life are evil and bring terrible suffering. But these verses assure believers that not only is their God always present, but He is also at work on their behalf to bring good out of the devil's most evil designs. The text still brings peace into settings of heart-wrenching turmoil.

But verse 28 should not be treated in isolation from the following two verses. These three verses are making the point that when God calls and the believer accepts, the life that follows is a life lived in God's hands. The passage speaks of those whom God called and foreknew and predestined and justified and glorified. Now, for God to "call" or even to "justify" us raises no problems and brings no debate. But at the word *foreknew*, eyebrows go up, and at the word *predestined*, alarm bells go off. We must get freedom of choice in there somewhere. But it's not really in there because it doesn't belong in there. If Paul is listing different aspects of the Christian's calling, they are all being viewed, not from the side of the Christian's freedom of choice, but from the side of God's pervasive grace. Sometimes Paul spoke this way to stress the sovereignty and power of God, but here his thrust was to bring peace and assurance to troubled, suffering believers. Accordingly, Paul spoke about how not only the believers' past was in God's mind, but their future as well. That is why he put the term *glorified* into a dramatic aorist tense, a literary technique by which a writer can indicate that a future event is so certain it can be spoken of as if it were already past. Paul's many exhortations to persevere, to "*continue* in his kindness; otherwise you too will be cut off" (11:22, emphasis supplied), which are scattered through many of his letters, make it evident that human freedom was an important part of his thinking and his theology. But in Romans 8 his stress was on divine planning so that discouraged, afflicted Christians can know that the God who called them will see them all the way through. It was Paul's practice to speak sometimes with human freedom in view and sometimes with the divine sovereignty uppermost; but rarely did he explain just which emphasis he was giving. Here, the all-important intermediate steps of human response or freedom would actually have detracted from his line of reasoning, which was to show how, from start to finish, God is at work at every stage in the call and spiritual development of the believer. Regarding such a divine initiative, the word *predestined* in verse 29 is not too strong. No personal salvation will take place by accident. Whoever will be saved will be called of God into that saving relationship—the initiative has always been God's, and He will not abandon us until we stand glorified before Him.

Which brought Paul to the glorious climax of wonder that closes this chapter. It is all so unbelievable that Paul had to strain to put it in words—"How can I say this?" (31). He seems moved both by the unfathomable love of God and the difficulty of trying to explain it. He fell back on the technique he had already used so much, reasoning from the greater to the lesser; from the obvious to the not so obvious. Since God has already sacrificed His Son for us, is there anything He won't do? Having paid the enormous debt, He will easily handle the nickels and dimes (32). Furthermore, since God is the One who has done all this, who would be so crazy as to challenge Him? And remember, it is no less than Christ Himself who now stands in our place at His Father's right hand. So it is settled. If anything is greater than conquerors, it's us (37), and no force in the entire universe can change that.

What more can Paul say?

Additional readings on chapter 12

Supplementary reading can be done from the sources listed at the end of chapter 10.

Chapter
Thirteen

The Role of Israel

Romans 9-11

Chapter 9—The role of Israel and the sovereignty of God

When an only child suddenly gets a sibling, adjustments are often painful. When Paul went about preaching that God's salvation was intended for Gentiles as well as for Jews (Acts 28:28), it was as if the privileged, only child suddenly had a sister. For generations, the idea that God had a "most favored nation" was taken for granted by many Jews. Now a noisy and influential preacher was traveling everywhere announcing that it wasn't so. At least that is the way the debate comes to us through the pen of Paul. And the emotions stirred were deeper and more gripping than we latter-day Gentiles can imagine. Paul's recent stress on the lost condition of all people ("The whole world may be held accountable to God," 3:19), as well as on the all-inclusiveness of God's grace ("He will justify the circumcised . . . and the uncircumcised," 3:30), posed a problem of great weight for Jews. Given such universalism, what was the meaning of Old Testament history? Did not such a gospel nullify the entire Abrahamic covenant? How was it possible to maintain any meaning in God's promises to Abraham and his offspring and at the same time accept the unrestricted gospel of Romans 1-8? The problem surfaced briefly in chapter 3:1-9, but for some reason, Paul did not go on to explain the issue fully. So now he proceeded to explain his earlier reference to the Jews' advantages (see 3:2; 9:4, 5) and then showed how his phrase "to the Jew first" (1:16) could still be true.

The poor treatment Paul received at the hands of the Jews, together with the consistently negative response of so many Jews to the Christian story, made it appear that either the gospel or the God of Abraham was wrong. Although Paul never really ceased appealing to Jews, his special ministry to the "uncircumcised" (Gal. 2:7) caused many Jews to wonder whether God was being true to His promises to Abraham. They seemed to reason that anything other than salvation for the Jews meant that God's word had failed. Paul quickly rejected such a premise. "It is not as though the word of God had failed" (6). The failure lay in the Jews' idea of their solidarity with Abraham. They had interpreted God's promises to Abraham in a narrow, literalistic way— they had, in effect, put God in a box. Paul summarily broke open the box with his assertion, "Not all are children of Abraham because they are his descendants" (7). The term *Israelite* means not bloodline or tradition, but a "circumcision of heart." At the same time, Paul's anguish of heart for his "kinsmen by race" (3) is obvious in that he so consistently approached "the Jew first" (Acts 14:1; 16:13; 17:1, 10; 18:4; Rom. 1:16; 2:9, 10).

At this point, one might expect Paul to expound more fully on the phrase "circumcision of the heart," and explain what put a Jew in that select group of *true* Jews. Instead, he turned his attention to the sovereign freedom of God to act in His own way, apart from any human expectations. His Old Testament illustration was transparent—Esau and Jacob should have been equals, with Esau getting the usual birthright privileges granted the firstborn. Instead, God made a distinction between them before they were born— before they had performed any deeds, good or bad, upon which a judgment could be made. In fact, God reversed the normal order of things by asserting that " 'the elder [should] serve the younger' " (12). Clearly, God is free to choose and to act in His own way, even if His action seems to fly in the face of human expectations and logic. Actually, such a view of God's sovereignty is in accord with the Old Testament conception of God. Israel of old felt perfectly comfortable with the thought that God had selected them for lofty purposes and Edom for ignoble ones. They viewed Moses as an example of God's mercy and Pharaoh as an example of His anger. So if Paul presented God as One who is entitled to act in an arbitrary manner, there should be no complaint from those with Israelite roots. Paul frequently isolated one aspect of the divine activity without carefully balancing it by its logical opposite. Thus, when we draw theological conclusions from his words, we should be careful to take into account any balancing logic, even if it can only be found in some other context.

A superficial observer who looks at Romans 9 will see a God who cares nothing for human response. He makes arbitrary decisions for His own inscrutable reasons, and if human bafflement results, so be it. But when we begin drawing theological conclusions, it is important to balance this picture of divine sovereignty with the many Pauline references elsewhere that imply divine love and human freedom. Also, we do well to notice that Paul did not speak in this chapter of selection to eternal life or eternal destruction. His main point here seems to have been that if God should act in an arbitrary fashion, no Jew who is steeped in Old Testament history has any right to complain.

At the same time, love for Jacob and hatred for Esau (13) sounds unusually harsh. However, we should not attach to the term *hatred* the loathing and disgust we usually give it. In that time it was "simply a way of saying that Esau was not the object of God's electing purpose" (Everett F. Harrison, *Romans*, vol. 10 of *The Expositor's Bible Commentary* [Grand Rapids, Mich.: Zondervan, 1976], p. 105). The word is similarly used in Luke 14:26, where Jesus said that discipleship involves "hatred" of one's own family members. Here the meaning should be softened to mean that family members are in no way to come between a person and his decision to follow Christ.

Another sometimes-troubling passage is the reference in verses 14-18 to Pharaoh's hardheartedness and God's role in making him that way. Whatever else the passage teaches, one paramount lesson is that God can be glorified, not only through those like Moses who serve Him, but also through those like Pharaoh who oppose Him. The problem is the source of that hostile spirit. Did God actually bring Pharaoh to this moment in history only to harden his heart and ultimately destroy him?

It is interesting to note that although there are several references in Exodus to Pharaoh hardening his own heart (see chapter 7:13, 22; 8:15, 19, 32; 9:7, 35), Paul never mentioned them. But of course his purpose here was not to explain the mechanics of human free will, which is usually our preoccupation, but to emphasize God's sovereign freedom. In that setting, Pharaoh epitomizes the folly of human resistance. In addition, he stands as an illustration of the principle expressed in Romans 1:24-28, that sinners left to themselves deteriorate into greater and greater depravity. But through it all, Paul did not teach a double predestination whereby some are chosen by God for life and some are chosen for death.

But he came close by suggesting that a potter has absolute control over his clay. If he decides to make from one lump a beautiful vase and an ugly dog dish, the dish has no real basis for complaint. The text does not indicate that God really acts this way. It simply says that if He did, no human complaint would be valid. In actual practice, God's patience and restraint consistently impressed Paul. Even when God deals with the seemingly impenitent, His purpose is consistently redemptive, so that any and all who turn to Him will be accepted by Him (2:4). Thus, when Paul referred to the objects of "his wrath" (9:22), he had in mind those who have chosen to turn away from God's mercy and have remained hardened to the gospel.

Paul next turned to the Assyrian invasion in Isaiah's time to illustrate, from one incident, two lessons that Paul's contemporary Jews needed to hear—God ultimately passes judgment on those who disobey, but He simultaneously shows His mercy by saving a remnant and inviting Gentiles to accept Him (27, 30). However, Paul went one step further.

He saw in that Old Testament incident a picture of a greater deliverance—the deliverance now available in Christ (33).

Chapter 10—Israel's failure to respond

While chapter 10 adds a few details to the explanation of Israel's failure, there is not a clear break in the reasoning between 9:33 and 10:1-4. In fact, in that passage, Paul explained what sets apart lost Jew from saved Gentile.

The former clung to righteousness by works, while the latter acknowledged the utter necessity of faith. In such a context, the statement in 10:4 that "Christ is the end of the law" fits perfectly. It does not mean, as some have charged, that Christ either abolished the law or that He fulfilled it so that it is no longer necessary. Here the train of thought has to do with works-righteousness versus faith-righteousness. Accordingly, Christ put an end to any kind of law/works-righteousness. Paul had already made clear (3:31) that the law as an objective guide for Christians was not abolished. But as a means of right standing with God, no amount of law keeping will suffice. Christ has put an end to any such thinking. Unfortunately, not all will see and accept it, so in 4b Paul added that it will happen only for those who believe.

But then 10:5 sounds as if in Moses' time, a person could actually attain righteousness by keeping the law. A closer examination of the context of Leviticus 18:5, however, suggests that God did not approve of salvation by works but was simply promising a blessing upon obedience. But Paul often drew on the words of the Old Testament to help him make a point quite different from that found in the original passage. Such was actually a Rabbinic method of interpretation. In any case, Paul's meaning in verses 5-9 is quite clear—salvation in Christ is now available and is as close as the breath it takes to confess Him. Human striving is pointless, since He is the One who has bridged the gap.

But the story of Jesus was so unique and incredible that perhaps the Jews' failure to respond was the fault of poor communication. If a person didn't hear right, is it possible no messenger was sent? Or, if someone was sent, did the hearer misunderstand? Paul shredded those objections by a series of Old Testament quotes that make two essential points: (1) the message had indeed been sent to Israel, but she disbelieved, and (2) since the Gentiles heard and responded favorably, the Jews could not plead ignorance or misunderstanding. Israel's problem was simple—they were " 'a disobedient and contrary people' " (21).

Chapter 11—A remnant of Israel will be saved

If a person receives a beautiful gift but refuses to open it, did the giver of the gift succeed or fail? God freely chose Israel for high privilege and responsibility (chapter 9) only to have Israel fail to appreciate the honor (chapter 10). In chapter 11, Paul turned to the resulting question: Did God fail in His endeavor? Is it possible that Israel's hardness of heart might ultimately thwart the purposes of God?

Paul began his answer to this question by reminding his readers of a point he made in 9:27 and repeated in 11:5, that at the center of Israel was the "true Israel" or "remnant." In other words, even though many in Israel rejected God's mercy, not all turned a deaf ear. A faithful remnant remained (4, 5). Just as Elijah had felt all alone in his service for God, so Paul may have felt lonely and hurt as he thought of how few of his fellow Israelites responded to the gospel. But lest someone think that because good people make good choices, they are the ones who get into the remnant, Paul made clear that inclusion in that choice group is not due to better works, but to grace (6). And those who failed lost out because they were hardened and became blind and deaf (7-10). How could God "harden" and "blind" them and then judge them?

Such terms once again raise the issue of human choice and freedom. As stated in connection with Romans 8:29, 30, Paul said too much elsewhere about human choice and about God's conditional judgment (see 11:22) to allow the terms here to take on their harshest implications. Instead, he used quotes from Isaiah 29 and Deuteronomy 29 to add the weight of the Old Testament to the argument he stated earlier (1:24-32)—that when people do not use their God-given faculties to perceive His truths, when they freely choose to turn against Him, He ultimately gives them up to the consequences of their choosing. This in turn becomes a process of "hardening."

But back to the earlier question, Was God's purpose completely thwarted? Paul's leadoff question in verse 11 implies a partial answer to that question. The NIV translation catches the thought—"Did they stumble so as to fall beyond recovery? Not at all!" Paul asserted that Israel's loss was not a total fall for two reasons. First, the failure of Israel as a nation was inextricably linked with the gospel to the Gentiles. In fact, in Paul's language, it is as if the one leads automatically to the other. In that sense the Gentiles' belief was actually a benefit that accrued from Israel's unbelief. This then led to the second positive outcome—when Israel saw the entrance of the Gentiles into God's plans and purposes, she would become jealous and, even if through questionable motives at first, would return to God and be accepted (11, 12, 15).

> The reason for Israel's being hardened in its rebellion against God's Son? Grace! Grace for gentiles, and finally, grace for Israel as well! God's plan, says Paul, runs from God choosing Israel, to his hardening Israel to save gentiles, and then to his saving gentiles in order finally to save Israel. . . . Hardening cannot alter the final purpose of God's election, which is grace (Paul J. Achtemeier, *Romans*, Interpretation: A Bible Commentary for Teaching and Preaching Series [Atlanta: John Knox Press, 1985], pp. 188, 189).

In Paul's following explanation he mixed his metaphors freely. But whether the figure is dough or first fruits (16) or wild olive branches (17), the thought is really quite clear—at the center was a small but believing group of Jews. Even if most of the branches (unbelieving Jews) were broken off, life was flowing through the roots. God did not completely abandon all Jews. But by their belief, Gentiles (the wild olive shoot, verse 17), were, in effect, grafted into the parent tree. The result was a hybrid melding of two into "one new [person] in place of the two" (Eph. 2:15).

Paul then gave counsel to each of these groups. Since the story of Christ develops out of, and is a natural fulfillment of, the Old Testament, Gentiles who come to have faith dare not think in arrogant ways about the Jews and their history. The root supports the branches, not vice-versa (18). So Gentiles should not "boast over the branches." Proud Gentile-Christians faced the same danger as hardhearted Jews, for "if God did not spare the natural branches, neither will he spare you" (21).

And to some bewildered Jews still pondering the meaning of their fractured hopes, Paul highlighted in verse 23 the persistent mercy and grace of God that would still accept penitent Jews. In fact, the conversion of Gentiles was so "contrary to nature" that it would be more in keeping with nature to graft back in the "natural branches" (Jews). Accordingly, Paul admitted in verse 25 that the hardening of *part* of Israel was indeed a mystery, but he assured his readers that "all Israel will be saved" (26). He had just said that God did not spare some of the natural branches! How could he then say that all Israel would be saved? If we view this as an unconditional promise, we must admit that it stands in hopeless contradiction with the immediate context. It is more reasonable to assume that Paul had in mind the salvation of a true *remnant* of Israel in all generations. Whether in Israel or in the Gentile world, it has always been faith that saves, and in this context of encouragement to Jews, Paul underscored the fullness of Israel's return. All those of faith, all the *true* Israelites, will be saved. To make the "all" of verse 26 into some kind of universalism whereby every Jew will be converted is surely an irresponsible interpretation. Accordingly, Paul's statement here is not unlike the modern-day assertion, "The *church* will be triumphant."

In chapter 11:32 Paul again offered the reminder that mercy is only meaningful when set against disobedience. In no way can Paul's words be used to support universalism. Always the context has to determine the scope of the words, and here the context relates to the differing roles and responses of Jews and Gentiles. Just as verses 30, 31 do not mean that all Gentiles and all Jews were totally unresponsive, so verse 32 does not mean that all, *without exception*, will be saved. Rather, it means that without distinction between Jew and Gentile, all who partake of His grace will be shown mercy. That assurance of unqualified and dependable mercy prompted Paul to burst forth into another hymn of wonder, reminiscent of the praise that concludes chapter 8. Who can possibly fathom a God like our God—who, in the face of disobedience and hardness of heart, can still show mercy and bring salvation.

Fourteen

Practical Concerns of the Transformed Life

Romans 12-16

Chapter 12—The sanctification theme

Faith in God and acceptance of His salvation are first grasped by the mind, then professed in words, then lived out in the life. Chapter 12 focuses on that last aspect. The earlier chapters of Romans dealt with the theological and philosophical aspects of conversion and righteousness by faith. Chapters 6-8 deal briefly with the postbaptismal experience, but again, it is largely from a theoretical viewpoint. In chapter 12 Paul focused more directly on the practical results on human behavior of the inner changes he discussed in earlier chapters.

When one thinks of the practical aspects of Christian behavior, it is essential to remember that there must be a natural connection between the *act* of faith (belief/justification), and the *life* of faith (Christian living/sanctification). In chapters 12-15 Paul gave several examples of what practical Christian living should look like. While justification by faith is often felt to be the primary teaching of Romans, Paul did not ignore the importance of practical Christian behavior. But he did not always develop his arguments in a perfectly balanced fashion. Since he was often reacting to local church problems, it should not be surprising that his emphasis was frequently one-sided. So in both Galatians and Romans, as the Christian church attempted to free itself from the legalism of Rabbinic Judaism, it is understandable that Paul should spend an inordinate amount of time on faith. But the amount of space devoted to a given topic is not the only factor that determines its importance.

As mentioned earlier, Romans was written to a church Paul had not visited, so it was not the same reactionary type of writing that we find in some of his other letters. This may explain why it has more balance than most. Still, the balance is often missed, for chapters 12-15 seem overshadowed by chapters 3-8. Also, understanding the transformation/sanctification process discussed in these later chapters is often more difficult for contemporary Christians than understanding the conversion experience.

First, Paul made clear (2) that the transformation process is a revolutionary change at the very center of our consciousness—our mind. Furthermore, the word *renewal* is an "action noun" that suggests the process must be continuous. It is not a sudden, once-for-all experience, but a process of thinking—of reaffirming. Furthermore, this process must constantly go forward in the midst of an opposing influence—"this world." It is clearly inadequate to think of the Christian life as total serenity with no opposing factors. But neither is Christianity lived successfully only by those with unusually high capacities of willpower or mental concentration. Always there is the reminder that the Christian's life arises out of the "faith which God has assigned him" (3). The tasks associated with Christian living overwhelm us only as we forget this reassuring promise—every assignment God hands out is accompanied by the necessary "measure of faith." It is when we ignore the faith relationship and attempt Christian behavior solely through willpower that failure and despair set in.

The remaining verses in chapter 12 are devoted to the variety of gifts God has distributed throughout the church—all of which have a very practical sound to them. Although the works described do not make up a Christian experience, a Christian experience will bear such fruit. In other words, it is not wrong or legalistic to expect Christian thought and experience to manifest themselves in Christian behavior.

Chapter 13—The Christian relates to his community

In a time when Christian groups were small and either misunderstood or held in contempt by those in authority, the subject of Christian-government relationships was undoubtedly a sensitive one. In chapter 13 Paul plunged directly into the problem of the Christian's relationship to his community. Apparently it was unclear to many new believers just how they could be loyal to God and at the same time obey any of the laws of a pagan ruler. The Christian has loyalties to two communities—the church community and all it represents, and the civil community. Just how to deal with the inevitable tensions between the two was a serious concern. It still is. But Paul's counsel suggests that those tensions need not be disastrous. In fact, the Christian has an obligation to defuse as much of the tension as possible. Thus, Paul argued that a Christian should be a good citizen and support the powers of government (1), even though in his day they must have been entirely pagan.

But it must be remembered that Paul was speaking to a specific situation (the Roman authorities were, at that point, reasonably tolerant toward Christians), yet he was using very general terms to set forth a general principle. He did not attempt to protect his generalities by discussing exceptions to the rule. The issue of if and when to resist a despotic, murderous ruler does not come into Paul's discussion at all. Unquestionably, the early church felt that when the realm of personal conscience is invaded by the state, the Christian must stand for God against man (Acts 5:29), but at other times, the obligations of good citizenship must not be taken lightly. A few years later, when John wrote Revelation, the activities of the government had changed considerably, and his language was much different from Paul's (compare Rom. 13:1 with Rev. 18:2, 3). But the principles of Romans 13:1-7 are not thereby destroyed. Paul clearly asserted that all human power is derived from God, and whether or not a human ruler acknowledges that fact, we Christians know it and can thus respect and show honor to the one who stands as God's representative. Exceptions to Paul's generality will continue to be debated, but his rule is still a good one—under *normal* circumstances, the Christian has the responsibility of being a good citizen.

Chapters 14 and 15—Loving tolerance— the guide to interpersonal relationships

The problem of Christians getting along with other Christians is not exactly a latter-day development. In chapter 14 Paul tackled head-on a couple of emotional issues that obviously stirred deep feelings among the Christians in Rome and probably elsewhere. The question at issue—when convictions conflict, how can love be served? When I abhor what you approve, how is compromise to be effected? At the very outset, Paul used the term *weak* to refer to the person who has scruples about his diet, and he counseled the strong person to be careful in his treatment of the "weak." To put it concisely, Paul's subject in chapter 14 is the liberated Christian's treatment of one who is not so liberated.

Unfortunately, while that is the topic, the specific examples he used are so emotion-laden that they tend to get all the attention, and the larger topic of tolerance and acceptance is often neglected or missed completely. Actually, the examples cited—dietary scruples and ceremonial feast days— were personal matters, and, by themselves, were probably morally neutral. But a Christian's treatment of another Christian is a serious matter of right or wrong. To put it another way, Christian faith brings freedom, but that freedom must always be limited by the larger issue of responsibility and concern for others. With a slightly different example (meat sacrificed to idols), Paul taught the same truth in 1 Corinthians 8.

Although Paul's plea for tolerance here strikes a somewhat softer note than that sounded in Galatians 4:11 ("I am afraid I have labored over you in vain"), the problems were similar. The Galatian Judaizers were apparently teaching that certain rituals were necessary for salvation, thereby destroying the essence of the gospel. Under such circumstances, Paul's severe language to them would be no surprise. The "weak" believers in Rome probably felt that their scrupulous behavior at least helped to bring them into favor with God, but they may not have been pushing their views as vigorously as the Galatians—hence Paul's milder tone. Still, the convictions of the "weak" were apparently deep enough that they were making an issue of them, which in turn was drawing fire from the "strong." In verse 3, Paul advised those on each side to avoid making an issue of the matter. "Let not him who eats despise him who abstains," he said, "and let not him who abstains pass judgment on him who eats; for God has welcomed him." In verse 4, he addressed both sides when he said, "Who are you to pass judgment on the servant of another?"

At first reading, it sounds as if the problem in Rome was the long-standing conflict between Jewish law and Christian freedom. While that may have been a factor, the regulations Paul mentioned went beyond Jewish law, for the idea of eating only vegetables was not a part of that law. In addition to personal preference, religious asceticism (self-denial for divine approval) may have prompted this brand of vegetarianism. Even if the vegetarianism itself was not "Jewish," the problem may have developed roughly along Jew-Gentile lines, in that the more scrupulous persons were those who, if not Jews, were at least under some Jewish influences, while the "stronger brethren" would likely have been either Gentiles or persons who clearly understood the gospel as Paul presented it to Gentiles.

Even given such a background, it sounds in verse 5 as if Paul threw all unanimity to the wind when he said that each person must be "fully convinced in his own mind." However, Paul was not advocating a "do your own thing" approach to Christian living. Rather, he was saying that all religious practice must have the weight of conscience behind it. Meaningful Christian behavior must be prompted by personal conviction, not mere verbal instruction. Mere conformity to a code of conduct means little. Furthermore, in addition to acting on the basis of personal conviction, the Christian lives his or her life with reference to the Lord and makes decisions with that reference in mind (6). So if both the one who abstained and the one who ate did so out of personal conviction and also as serving the Lord, then each should practice tolerance toward the other. At this juncture, who was right and who was wrong is beside the point. If both were the Lord's, they answered to Him, not to one another (8, 10).

The "day" Paul referred to in verses 5, 6 deserves careful treatment. It should be noted that the term is used in close connection with dietary scruples that have little connection to any divine obligation. But such is not the case with the weekly day of worship, which comes to us as a Creation ordinance, designed to help keep us in touch with our Maker. The weekly holy day did not first exist in the Mosaic law. It existed from the very beginning of human history (Gen. 2:2, 3) and has behind it the authority of a divine decree. The sanctity of that particular holy day was such that no casual reference, such as that of 14:5, would be adequate to diminish its great importance. But there was growing uncertainty about the importance of certain Jewish feasts and "holy days." Paul himself seemed unclear about certain Jewish practices (Acts 21:20-27), so it is certain that many believers, especially those of Gentile backgrounds, were unsure about the necessity or meaning of ceremonial "high days." Again, Paul did not rule on their moral value (thus indicating that he did not have in mind the weekly Sabbath) but suggested that this also was a personal issue which should be decided without the pressure and intolerance that was causing such unnecessary strife.

In verses 13-23 Paul directed his remarks to the strong brother, who was warned of the effect his example could have on the weak, by leading him to go against what his conscience told him. The issue was not the details of a proper diet, but the relationship between rights and responsibility. His statement in verse 14 shows that Paul considered himself a "strong" brother who knew that the food in question was not, of itself, good or evil, clean or unclean. But he knew that those categories were of great importance because they were based on inner convictions, from which the consciences of his readers either condemned or acquitted them. He also knew that the power of example and influence is very strong and thus carries heavy responsibility. Thus, "strong" believers, who knew that the kingdom of God does not mean food or drink (17), might, by their example, lead a weaker believer to go against his conscience, thereby injuring the weak believer. Such behavior is unloving (15), and that was the real source of Paul's concern here.

In verse 17 Paul lifted the discussion above food and drink and reminded the Roman Christians that they were members of a higher kingdom. The deeper concerns of life have to do with spiritual realities, which form the basis of "peace and joy in the Holy Spirit." Keeping this in mind will bring about that spirit of unity among the members which is far more important than a narrow insistence upon unqualified liberty by some. When concern for the larger "work of God" (20) is paramount, petty preoccupations with food and drink melt away, and the resulting peace contributes to the mutual growth of all concerned. So Paul's strong appeal to these believers who were arguing over morally neutral issues was to come together "in such harmony . . . that . . . with one voice," they might glorify "the God and Father of our Lord Jesus Christ" (15:5, 6).

Conclusion of the letter

From 15:14 to 16:27 Paul turned to personal reflections. He spoke of his personal desire to visit the Romans and of his dreams to extend the gospel even to Spain (15:24) and beyond. In chapter 16 he sent personal greetings to a long list of friends, who had apparently moved to Rome from many of the cities he had previously visited. So the letter that is the most systematically theological of all Paul's letters ends on a very warm, personal note.

Additional readings on chapter 13

1. James D. G. Dunn, *Romans 9-16, Word Biblical Commentary* (Dallas: Word, 1988).
2. Supplementary reading can also be done in the works cited at the end of chapter 10.

Chapter
Fifteen

The Prison Epistles

Ephesians, Colossians, Philemon, Philippians

Hardships and humiliation became a way of life for Paul. Midway through his third missionary journey (2 Cor. 11:21-29), his beatings, shipwrecks, and varied other assaults sound more like a man on the run than a man of the cloth. Given the implacable hostility of his enemies, it is not too surprising that in four of his letters (Eph. 3:1; 4:1; Phil. 1:7, 13, 14; Col. 4:18; Philem. 1, 9), he makes specific reference to his chains or bonds. In other words, he was writing from some kind of imprisonment. These four letters have come to be known as the prison epistles. The exact nature of the imprisonment is unclear, but some kind of detention is obvious. Of the four, Ephesians, Colossians, and Philemon are closely linked in time and place of writing, as Tychicus delivered both Colossians and Ephesians (Col. 4:7; Eph. 6:21), and Colossians 4:9 mentions Onesimus, who was the bearer of Philemon. In addition, Archippus is greeted in both Colossians 4:17 and Philemon 2. Clearly, these three letters can claim the same approximate time and place of authorship. Philippians does not have the same connecting links of names, so it may have been written somewhat later. Also, in Philemon 22, Paul's release seems rather distant, while in Philippians 1:25 he speaks as if it is imminent, which suggests a later date for Philippians.

Time and place of imprisonment

Nowhere in the epistles did Paul clearly specify where he was imprisoned. Luke made reference to a two-year Caesarean (Acts 23:32-35; 24:27) and a two-year Roman imprisonment (Acts 28:16, 30, 31), but Caesarea does not seem a likely place for the writing of these epistles. In both Ephesians (6:19, 20) and Colossians (4:3, 4), Paul asked an interest in the believers' prayers that he might be a faithful witness in spite of his bonds. Such a statement could apply to either Caesarea or Rome, but it sounds a little more like Rome, since Luke already mentioned that that imprisonment allowed Paul to preach and teach "quite openly and unhindered" (Acts 28:31). No such statement is made about his Caesarean imprisonment. In addition, in Philemon 22, Paul expressed the hope that he would soon be released to visit Philemon, and such a release from the Caesarean imprisonment seems most improbable. After all, he had already appealed to Caesar, so going to visit Philemon after his release was not likely to happen. On the other hand, if his appeal to Caesar went well, it is conceivable he could have been released from that imprisonment.

An Ephesian imprisonment has also been suggested, but the evidence is very slender. For three years in the midst of his third missionary trip, Paul lived in Ephesus (Acts 20:31), during which time he wrote the two letters to the Corinthians. In those letters he made cryptic references that some have interpreted as referring to a possible Ephesian imprisonment. In 1 Corinthians 15:32 he alluded to fighting with "wild beasts" in Ephesus, and in 2 Corinthians 11:23 he mentioned "far more imprisonments." However, the "wild beasts" phrase is often viewed as figurative, much like his "fierce wolves" in Acts 20:29. Also, his Roman citizenship would have made unlikely any persecution that included wild animals.

The most likely time and place for the writing of these letters is the first Roman imprisonment (Acts 28:30, 31), which dated from A.D. 61-63. Paul's reference to the "praetorian guard" and "Caesar's household" (Phil. 1:13; 4:22), along with his allusion to a possible death sentence (Phil. 2:17), all point more toward Rome than toward any other setting. In addition, the presence of Luke with Paul (Col. 4:14) argues for Rome, as it is certain that Luke accompanied Paul to Rome (Acts 28:14), but it is quite uncertain that he was with Paul in Ephesus.

Ephesians

As hardships go, Paul's first Roman imprisonment was pretty tame, as he continued to teach and preach and even entertain friends (Acts 28:30, 31). When one such friend, Tychicus, a native of Ephesus, was about to head back east, Paul took advantage of the occasion by sending with him a letter to the believers in that region. In most English Bibles this letter is labeled, "To the Ephesians." However, one of the most surprising characteristics of the Ephesian letter is the general nature of the language and instruction in it. Since, as far as we know, Paul had lived in Ephesus longer than in any other city, a letter to that church might well have contained a number of warm, personal greetings. Instead, Paul's language is so general that it seems almost distant. It is hard to imagine Paul saying to his Ephesian friends and co-workers, "I have heard of your faith in the Lord" (1:15). In fact, throughout the epistle, he made not a single reference to his former work among them. Also, in contrast with Colossians and Philemon, Ephesians has no greetings from any of Paul's companions, though both Timothy and Aristarchus were well known to the believers in that city (Acts 19:22, 29; 1 Cor. 4:17).

Consequently, the suggestion has been made that the letter was sent out originally as a circular letter, intended for the general instruction of several churches, and either began or ended up with the Ephesians. The suggestion is underscored by Paul's suggestion to the Colossians that they send their letter on to the Laodiceans and also that they read the one he had sent to the Laodiceans (Col. 4:16).

The view that Ephesians was a circular letter is also one explanation for the missing destination in the earliest manuscripts. In a few of the reliable manuscripts, the words *in Ephesus* are missing from 1:1, resulting in an awkward gap— as if the city name was to be filled in by the messenger who was delivering the letter when he got there. Numerous recent translations, in their attempts to be true to the early manuscripts, have left out the destination, with a less than ideal result: "To the saints who are . . . also faithful in Christ Jesus." The rather prominent position of Ephesus in Paul's labors may have been the reason why that name became attached to the letter. Still, the precise details of the letter's destination may never be solved.

Occasion and purpose

In keeping with the idea that the letter was intended for more than one audience, Ephesians does not appear to be a strong reaction to any one local problem. Its theme is more lofty and general than that of the other epistles, in that it focuses on the universality of the church and its need for unity and beauty as it comes to realize its true calling as the unblemished bride of Christ (5:27). If there is one recurring theme, it is the call for unity—a unity that embraces both Jew and Gentile and makes of them one new person, a Christian (2:15). The source of that unity is never in question. It is always "to unite all things in him" (1:10).

Chapter 1—God's love planned ahead

The primary message of Ephesians 1 is simple and to the point: The incredible plan for reconciling sinful human beings with God was formulated well in advance—"before the foundation of the world" (1:4). Before getting into the details of the reconciliation, Paul spoke of God's saving "purpose" and how He "destined us in love to be his sons" (5; see also 11, 12). It is one thing to be the object of a person's love, but it adds emphasis and poignancy to be told that a loving plan preceded your very existence. Paul seems to have felt that there was no more emphatic way he could speak of God's grace in Christ than by emphasizing that it was all in the mind of God long before the fact.

Chapter 2—Salvation summarized

People in a hurry like their books condensed and their theology simple and summarized. Ephesians 2 is for them. If one chapter encapsulates the whole alienation/reconciliation story of the gospel, it is this one. It begins with the depressing picture of human lostness and depravity ("dead through the trespasses," verse 1), and it ends with a portrait of the beautiful spiritual household that the reconciliation through Christ has created.

This comprehensive chapter contains an even more concise expression of the gospel, which is absolutely brilliant in its brevity and clarity. A million words have been written to clarify and explain the gospel, but none are so simple and complete as those in Ephesians 2:8-10: "By grace you have been saved through faith; and this is not your own doing, it is the gift of God—not because of works, lest any man should boast. For we are his workmanship, created in Christ Jesus for good works." The essence of righteousness by faith is hard to misread in this passage.

In the following verses Paul applied this expression of grace and faith to a particularly vexing problem of disunity among the Ephesians—the rift between Jew and Gentile. In Romans 11 he had spoken of the same problem under the figure of the root (Judaism), the broken-off branches (unfaithful Jews), and the wild olive shoot grafted in (Gentiles). Here he was a bit more direct, and in verses 11, 12 he reminded the Gentiles that they were separated from Christ and alienated from Israel, but had now been "brought near in the blood of Christ" (13). This reconciliation between Jew and Gentile was made possible by the breaking down of the "wall of hostility," which took place when Christ abolished in His flesh the "law of commandments and ordinances" (15). This last phrase is often interpreted to mean that since Christ's death fulfilled the types and symbols in the Jewish ceremonial system, that system was abolished and was thus no longer a barrier for Gentile converts.

At the same time, Christ's death did more than unite Jew and Gentile. Paul hastened to add that Christ's ultimate purpose was to "create . . . one new man in place of the two, so making peace, and [to] reconcile [them] both to God in one body through the cross" (15, 16). The plan was not that Gentiles now become full-fledged Jews, but that both could become Christians ("one new man"), and thus be reconciled, not simply to each other, but to God. In other words, the ultimate hostility was not between Jew and Gentile but between sinful humans and God. So when Paul said that the wall of hostility was broken down when Christ abolished the "law of commandments and ordinances," he must have had more in mind than the rituals of the Mosaic law. Abolishing the ceremonial law does not reconcile people to God. Ultimate reconciliation can happen only when the debt of sin (that is, our guilty indebtedness to the moral law) is cancelled. Although the passage does suggest that Christ's death did away with ceremonial barriers, it also suggests that the ultimate barrier, indebtedness to the moral law, was likewise broken down. The result is peace, both to those who were far off (Gentiles) and to those who were near (Jews). The reconciliation is complete.

Chapter 3—Paul's commission—to remove the unknown from the mystery of the gospel

Paul's lively and spontaneous style of writing jumps out in chapter 3. It appears that his primary concern started out as a prayer on behalf of the readers that they would experience more deeply the love of Christ and the power of the Spirit (19, 20). But as soon as he mentioned his imprisonment (1), he felt constrained to explain how he had come to his present position as a minister of this gospel. So verses 2-13 probably comprise an interruption of his original flow of thought, to which he returned in verse 14.

But throughout the reiteration of his call, he referred three times to the entire revelation experience as a mystery (3, 4, 9). Paul seems to like the connotation of the word *mystery*, since he used it repeatedly to speak of God's eternal plan to save the race. But for him, the actual mystery referred to God's plan in the past, for in Christ the mystery had been cleared up. Since Christ has come and died, people can, for the first time, "see what is the plan of the mystery hidden for ages in God who created all things" (9).

Chapter 4—A few practical implications for Christian living

The flak Paul got for being a theoretical, philosophical, impractical theologian was largely undeserved. Repeatedly, he addressed himself to all phases of practical Christian living. Ephesians 4 is one such passage. What could be more practical than for Christians to learn to live together in unity (1-6)? Such unity is not achieved through grit and determination, but by accepting the grace that has been granted to "each of us" (7). Through that grace God also gives a variety of gifts of the Spirit so that the collective body, the church, can grow (11-13). The list of gifts resembles those given elsewhere (Rom. 12:6-8; 1 Cor. 12:7-11, 28-30), yet each list has differences as well as similarities. Perhaps Paul was indicating that, since the spiritual needs of the various church groups were both similar and different, the need for unity was best served by allowing and even encouraging diversity of gifts.

Attempting to maintain a little faith and a little worldliness is impossible. Instead, Paul admonished believers to make a clean break with their past (22) so that their profession and practice could be in complete harmony. In verses 25-32 he gave more practical examples of how the resulting Christian unity will affect everything from anger to thievery to evil speaking. Clearly, genuine Christianity makes people nicer.

Chapters 5 and 6—Unity in Christ sweetens the church and sweetens the home

If some Christians fear that explicit directives about Christian behavior will push believers toward legalism, Paul did not. In fact, in these last two chapters of Ephesians he added several no-nonsense prohibitions to his sometimes-mild suggestions—"no filthiness, nor silly talk"; "no . . . impure man . . . has any inheritance"; "try to learn what is pleasing to the Lord"; "do not get drunk" (5:4, 5, 10, 18).

In chapters 5:21–6:4 Paul gave special attention to the unity of the home. It is a beautiful passage, which shows with what high esteem he regarded the marriage relationship. In fact, this brief section provides an important balance to the rather limited view of marriage that is sometimes gleaned out of 1 Corinthians 7. One can hardly take seriously Paul's analogy of a wife with the church that is without spot, wrinkle, or blemish (5:27) and hold that Paul had a low view of marriage in general and women in particular. Paul did teach that Christian wives should show the proper degree of respect to their husbands, but his stress on the husband's love for his wife is such that no couple who follows his counsel can have a serious problem with the matter of equality, which is such an important part of today's gender talk.

Some have been troubled that Paul did not call for the abolition of slavery and instead admonished slaves to be obedient to their masters and masters to be considerate of their slaves (6:5-9). However, he had already made it clear that the gospel is the great leveler that makes all people, including slaves and masters, equal before God (Gal. 3:28). But cultural practice often has to wait while the leavening influence of the gospel gradually permeates all levels of human behavior. Attempting to bring about an abrupt cultural change is often worse than futile, as it can cause premature polarizing of the people, so that the process of gradual change is actually halted. While the Christian should not acquiesce to conditions that are evil, he may, at times, have to be temporarily content to interject as much Christianity as possible into an evil situation and wait until the time is ripe for more radical change.

In verses 10-20 Paul concluded his instruction with the reminder that the Christian must practice his Christianity in the face of intense opposition. The Christian walk is no sham battle. The enemies are real, and the conflict is life or death. Consequently, the Christian cannot be lax in his preparation, and the proper armor will make the difference between success or failure, life or death.

Colossians

As mentioned earlier in this chapter, the time and place of the writing of Colossians was virtually the same as that of

Ephesians, so nothing further will be said on that issue here.

Destination

In Paul's day, the city of Colossae was a small town of west-central Asia Minor, about one hundred miles east of Ephesus. Its nearest neighbor town was Laodicea, about ten miles away, to which Paul made reference in chapter 4:16. Paul may have passed through that region on both his second and third missionary trips, but neither city is mentioned in Acts. Some speculate that Paul evangelized the area during his three-year stay in Ephesus on his third journey. However the gospel seed was first scattered, it is apparent from this letter that it had borne fruit, and Paul felt burdened to establish the church on a more firmly Christ-centered foundation.

Occasion and purpose

When Epaphras came calling on Paul, he brought good news and bad news. The good news of the believers' love in the Spirit is mentioned in 1:8, but the bad news of a spreading heresy is determined more indirectly by listening to the kind of instruction Paul sent in the Colossian letter. So the occasion of the letter was Paul's reaction to the news brought by Epaphras (1:7, 8). After a brief word of thanks for their faith and love, Paul launched into his purpose in writing to the Colossians, which was to combat the heresy that was gaining ground. He wanted to bring the believers back to the purity of his gospel. Because so much of Colossians seems to refer to aspects of this false teaching, some understanding of the heresy is important for a proper interpretation of several passages.

The Colossian heresy

The Colossian heresy had several facets. First, it is clear that some believers had slipped back into certain Jewish practices. The references to circumcision (2:11; 3:11), as well as to judgmental attitudes regarding the "festival," "new moon," and "sabbath" (2:16), indicate that Judaistic demands comprised part of the belief system that Paul was writing against. But there were also elements that went beyond anything in the Mosaic rituals. For example, in 2:18, 20-23, he berated their worship of angels as well as their practices of self-denial, which looked very pious on the outside, but were "of no value in checking the indulgence of the flesh" (23). Such elements arose, not out of Judaism or Christianity, but out of the philosophical speculations that were spreading throughout the land. By the second and third century, such ideas came to be more or less organized under the general term of *Gnosticism*. This loose-knit system of belief held that humans are caught up in a great spirit-matter dualism, in which there is constant conflict between *matter* (the body, which is evil) and *spirit* (the mystical, nonmaterial aspect of man, which is good). If a person will afflict his body, physically abusing himself, matter will be put down, and the spirit will thereby be exalted. This false teaching went on to deny that God (being spirit, and therefore good) could have any contact with matter (being evil). Consequently, there could be no such thing as God coming in human flesh. The humanity of Christ and His suffering on the cross were only appearances—they could not be real. In addition, Gnostics believed in a superior wisdom or knowledge (the Greek word for knowledge is *gnōsis*—hence, Gnosticism) for the privileged few. The masses were not included in this inner circle of elite ones who had the saving knowledge.

Needless to say, in all this philosophizing, Christ took a secondary place. He apparently was not denied, but He was dethroned. Thus, another element of the heresy was a pseudo-Christianity that accepted Christ in a depreciated form, not as the God-man. Apparently, the Colossians gave Him lip service, but they were not "holding fast to the Head" (2:19). Paul set out to vigorously disparage these false ideas by putting Christ back into the central position. In the process, he attacked aspects of Gnostic philosophy, Judaizing demands, and a distorted Christianity.

Chapter 1—The all-sufficient Christ

Following his usual greeting, Paul expressed his thanksgiving to the Colossians for what he had "heard of [their] faith in Christ" (4). This phrase, together with the statement in chapter 2:1 that he was striving for them because they had not seen his face, is evidence that Paul probably did not personally establish the church in Colossae. But that in no way detracted from his fervor.

In verses 9, 10 and again in 2:2, 3, Paul appears to have been attacking the idea of elitism that was so much a part of Gnosticism and was now affecting these Colossian Christians. An exclusive knowledge for the privileged few is rejected by Paul's assertion that in Christ there is true knowledge, and it is available to all—not just a select few. Similarly, in chapter 1:28 he spoke of warning "*every* man" and teaching "*every* man in *all* wisdom, that we may present *every* man mature in Christ." Surely some kind of exclusivism is under attack here.

As a rule, Scripture does not set out to prove God's existence or even to give extended arguments for the deity of Christ. But Colossians 1:15-20 does seem to be an exception to that rule. These verses comprise one of the most complete statements on the deity of Christ in the entire New Testament. It is hard to read this passage and not think about the way the Colossian heretics had depreciated the deity of Christ. This majestic passage leaves no room for a merely human Jesus or for a hierarchy of angel mediators between God and man. Christ is not only superior to all creation, but in Him dwells the fullness of God. Some scholars have suggested that the word *fullness* was a technical term for all the various powers that made up the angel hierarchies of the Gnostics. If so, that puts an additional thrust into Paul's description of the supremacy of Christ.

When Paul, in Colossians, touched on the reconciling work of Christ (21-23), he sounds very much like he did in Ephesians. Numerous passages in the two letters are strikingly similar. For example, in Ephesians 3:7-13 and Colossians 1:24-27, Paul spoke of his suffering; of his being called to be a minister; of his proclamation of the "mystery" once hidden, but now made known; and of his desire that the believers take courage from his suffering. Such similarity is understandable when we remember that both letters were written about the same time to people living in the same general area. The differences are likewise obvious, however. Colossians is much more specific in its attacks on heresy than is Ephe-sians, and its style is similarly direct and explicit, whereas Ephesians is softer and more general.

Chapter 2—Religious practice
apart from Christ is empty of meaning

A careful reading of Colossians quickly reveals that the insidious false teachings of the heretics were never far from Paul's mind. For example, when Paul juxtaposed the suffi-ciency of Christ with the inadequacy of human philosophies and rituals (6-23), he wanted his readers to understand that all religious thought and practice which does not have Christ at its center has little value. Conversely, in Christ, the Christian comes to "fulness of life," since He is the "head of all rule and authority" (10). As mentioned above, opponents of the gospel had mixed together a number of erroneous ideas, most of which arose out of Judaism, developing Gnosticism, and some corrupted aspects of Christianity. The terms in verse 8 (*philosophy, human tradition*) envision Gnostic leanings, while the references to circumcision (11) and the Sabbath (16) imply Judaizing influences. But Paul's directives are so intertwined that one gets the distinct impression he was not thinking of separate heresies but rather of a conglomerate of false teachings. If there was a central error, it must have been an inadequate view of Christ and His reconciling act. Whereas in 1:15-20 Paul empha-sized the deity and overall preeminence of Christ, in 2:9-15 he stressed the completeness of the reconciliation by re-minding believers that their sins were forgiven (13) when the legal bond ("handwriting of ordinances," KJV) was nailed to the cross and thereby cancelled (14).

What was nailed to the cross has been traditionally viewed by Adventists as the ceremonial laws of Moses. An alternate view that also agrees with Adventist theology is that the condemning aspects of the Decalogue were nailed to the cross. Since verses 13, 14 stress that cancelling the bond brought about forgiveness of sins, it sounds as if Paul had in mind more than termination of the ceremonies. The greatest achievement of Christ on the cross was not the termination of the ceremonies but the reconciling of sinful humans and a holy God. This happened when Christ freed us from the consequences of breaking the Decalogue. This act of Christ also stripped the evil powers of their authority and openly displayed the devil and his host as defeated (15). This interpretation of "handwriting of ordinances" (14, KJV) agrees with that given for the same terms when they are used in Ephesians 2:15, described earlier in this chapter. There, the surrounding context is slightly different, but the underlying issue is the same—reconciling lost humans to God.

The interpretation of verse 16 also rests upon the adequacy of Christ's sacrifice, which is why the verse begins with the word *therefore*. In this verse, it is clear that Jewish demands were posing a problem. When verses 16-19 are read as a unit, we can see that the Jewish rituals in question were being pushed ahead of Christ. Whatever interpretation we give to the words *festival, new moon, sabbath,* we must keep in mind that the people advocating them were "not holding fast to the Head" (19). Such religious rituals, however proper they might seem, were empty shadows compared to the substance—which was Christ (17). When viewed in this way, it is possible to see the sabbath here as a reference to the weekly Sabbath observance by some who were, at the same time, depreciating Christ.

Admittedly, this sounds a little scary to people who believe that the weekly Sabbath has always been a memorial of Creation and therefore unaffected by the death and resurrection of Christ. According to this view, the sabbaths of verse 16 can only refer to the ceremonial sabbaths that were scattered throughout the Jewish calendar. But other facts have a bearing on a correct interpretation of verses 16, 17. For example, throughout the Old Testament, ceremonial sabbaths were included under the term Paul used in verse 16 for "festival." This would mean that Paul said, "Festival [which included ceremonial sabbaths] . . . new moon . . . ceremonial sabbath." Also, whenever the Greek translation of the Old Testament uses the phrases "festival—new moon—sabbath," it consistently implies a logical sequence of time from yearly to monthly to weekly. Sometimes the order is reversed, but monthly is always in the middle. Such arguments make it appear that the sabbath Paul referred to in verse 16 was the weekly Sabbath.

As stated above, however, the verse is no threat to genuine Sabbath keepers if we remember that Paul was attempting to correct a heresy that dethroned Christ, not one that abolished the Sabbath. Paul's counsel here condemns any ritual, including the Sabbath, that separates people from Christ (19). This is the contrast he had in mind when he juxtaposed "shadow" and "substance" in verse 17. When these words are used together, the word for *shadow* never means "*fore*shadow," in the sense of anticipating. It only means emptiness, as compared to the substance or reality. But nothing is shadowy about the Sabbath. When it is truly observed, the believer is reminded of the divine Creator and of the beautiful rest from labor, both physical and spiritual, that belief in Christ entails. On the other hand, when religious practices are advocated by those who have relegated Christ to an inferior position, it is not surprising that the forthright, outspoken Paul would call all such practices empty shadows when compared to the substance, Jesus Christ.

There are various ways of depreciating the sacrifice of Christ, and self-deprivation is one. Humans are often determined to offer God their own self-sacrifice as partial payment for guilt and sin. This problem is clearly a part of the asceticism that comes into focus in verses 20-23. As mentioned above, some elements were no doubt Jewish, but the "self-abasement and severity to the body" of verse 23 sound more like the rigorous demands of Gnosticism than the expectations in Jewish law.

Chapters 3 and 4—Practical Christian living for those who have been raised with Christ

Because of the similarity between the last two chapters of Colossians and the last chapter of Ephesians, no further comments will be made at this point.

Philemon

The value of this little letter is not in its presentation of doctrine (there is none), but in its beautiful illustration of Christianity at work in a particularly difficult setting. Slavery, with all its inequities, was an integral part of the social structure of the time. Even middle-class homes often had six to eight slaves, and royalty usually had thousands. Rules for slaves varied, but they had few rights, and the penalty for escape was death if the master so chose.

It appears that Onesimus, a slave, had escaped from Philemon and fled to Rome, where he crossed paths with Paul and was captured by the power of the gospel. Paul, who was not always constrained by the rules of tact and verbal niceties (see Acts 13:10; 23:3; Gal. 5:12), was now a master of tact and diplomacy as he reasoned with Philemon to take back his former slave, who was now a brother in the faith. In the process, he was not above using psychological pressure (18, 19) as he reminded Philemon, "You owe me one" (19).

If the epistles concerned themselves solely with doctrinal instruction, this little letter would have no place among them. But since Paul was concerned with practice as well as theory, his admonition to Philemon about his repentant slave Onesimus was pertinent indeed. Still, Paul may have written many such personal letters, so it is legitimate to ask why this one was preserved. John Knox offers an intriguing suggestion. "If Onesimus was on his way back into slavery when Philemon was written, the question seems unanswerable. But if he was on his way out of slavery into Paul's service, an answer immediately suggests itself" (John Knox, "The Epistle to Philemon," in *The Interpreter's Bible*, ed. George A. Buttrick [New York: Abingdon, 1955], vol. 11, p. 557). Since Paul's co-workers and associates, like Timothy, Titus, and Silas, became leaders of various churches, it is fascinating that one of the epistles of Ignatius, written early in the second century, mentions that the bishop of the church at Ephesus was a man named Onesimus. Whether this was the same Onesimus mentioned in Philemon we cannot say, but this little personal letter makes clear that

Christianity was permeating the marketplace, not just the holy place.

Philippians

Introduction

On Paul's second missionary journey, he spent a very short time in the city of Philippi ("some days," Acts 16:12), during which time he and Silas were wrongfully imprisoned, then released by embarrassed officials (Acts 16:39). During their abbreviated stay, three notable conversion stories fill Luke's account in Acts 16—Lydia and her household, the girl with the spirit of divination, and the jailer and his household. When Paul and the others moved on, Luke stayed, and together with these few new Christians formed the nucleus of a church that Paul would again visit briefly on the return from his third missionary journey (Acts 20:6). Even though some of the names found in the preceding three letters have changed, it is widely believed that Paul wrote Philippians during his first Roman imprisonment, though perhaps a bit later than the others. But since the time is roughly the same as that of the preceding letters, more will not be said here about the historical setting.

Occasion and purpose

In Colossians it was Epaphras (1:7) who visited Paul and gave him occasion to write. Now it is Epaphroditus who pays him a visit and gives him an opportunity to write another letter. It seems the Philippian believers had sent Paul some gifts, and he wanted to thank them for their kindness. Thus his purpose in this letter was to express his appreciation and joy as he reflected on the Philippians' sincere love and support for him in his imprisonment. In addition, Epaphroditus, a good friend of many Philippians, had become gravely ill but had recovered, and Paul wanted to send him back to his friends, who had heard of his illness and had worried a great deal about him (2:26-30).

Theme

As the Preacher said, there is "a time to embrace, and a time to refrain from embracing" (Eccl. 3:5). When Paul wrote to the Galatians and to certain Corinthians, he pointedly refrained from embracing, but when he wrote this short letter to the Philippians, he "embraced" his readers all the way through. While all of Paul's letters except Galatians have some message of thanksgiving for the faith of the believers, Philippians continues that thanksgiving throughout the entire letter. From beginning to end, the letter flows on with a steady stream of thankful joy. The word *rejoice,* or words with that meaning, appears sixteen times in this short letter.

Chapter 1

As placid as things are in the letter, a ripple or two crop up. After a long section of pleasantries, the first unpleasant note (15-18) has to do with some competitive preachers—but they were in Rome, not Philippi. Apparently, these were fellow evangelists, not the Judaizers mentioned in chapter 3, for they were preaching Christ. Unfortunately, they were mean-spirited and petty, driven by self-serving motives. Although Paul was disappointed in their spirit, his attitude was almost philosophical as he stated that even if their motives were tainted, so long as Christ was preached, some good would result. Clearly, it was a matter of attitude, not content, or his words would not have been so tempered.

Given his imprisonment, it is not surprising that his physical circumstances were never far from Paul's thoughts. The seriousness of it all jerks into view in verses 20-26 as he suddenly spoke of death as a very near option. As he pondered his immediate future and realized that his appeal to Caesar could result in a death sentence, he viewed the possible outcomes with a certain equanimity. If he spoke of death in almost favorable terms, he was not turning against life. As a traveling evangelist, Paul experienced a series of traumas (2 Cor. 11:23-29), and for one whose daily life was in Christ, the prospect of imminent death was simply not that intimidating. But in spite of the way verse 22 sounds, Paul knew that the choice was not really his. In fact, his words should probably be translated, "What I really prefer, I cannot make known."

Some see in his "depart and be with Christ" an acceptance of death as the somewhat-friendly vehicle that would usher him directly into heaven. But he told the Corinthians that death was an enemy which would finally be destroyed (1 Cor. 15:26). In addition, he told them that at the last trumpet there would be a resurrection of the dead (1 Cor. 15:51, 52), and only at that future time would they "all be changed." Here in Philippians, Paul probably meant only that there were advantages to either of the options that faced him in the near future. Although he wasn't positive what would come (2:23), he seemed confident that his ministry was not yet over (1:25). But if it should be, he was just as confident that his next conscious existence would be with Christ.

Chapter 2
In a setting of admonitions toward unselfishness, Paul included in verses 5-11 a Christological statement that is as beautiful as any in the New Testament. Because of its rhythmical style, some have called it a hymn, and speculated that Paul borrowed it from some other early Christian literature. However, the evidence is divided, and since Paul himself occasionally soared into masterly prose (see Rom. 8:35-39; 1 Cor. 13), it is reasonable to view the passage as a beautiful illustration by Paul of Christ's unfathomable condescension.

Occasionally, a Christian group can develop an unhealthy dependence upon a favored leader, and in verse 12, Paul warned the Philippians not to allow that to happen. They were answerable to God, not to Paul, and it was with God they were to work out their salvation. Furthermore, when he said, "Work out your own salvation," Paul did *not* mean "work for" or "earn." Rather, he meant that the Christian must personally see that salvation becomes operational in his or her life. "Justification must be followed by the experiential aspects of sanctification, by which the new life in Christ is consciously appropriated and demonstrated" (Homer A. Kent, Jr., "Philippians," in *The Expositor's Bible Commentary*, ed. Frank Gaebelein [Grand Rapids, Mich.: Zondervan, 1978], vol. 11, p. 128). The essence of salvation is only in Christ, as verse 13 makes clear, but that fact must be daily acknowledged in our minds and hearts if our salvation is ultimately to be "worked out."

The remainder of the chapter is devoted almost entirely to warm personal observations, including a testimony to the deep affection Paul felt toward Timothy. Paul did not have children of his own, but his expressions of love and caring for Timothy show how much his various children in the faith meant to him.

Chapter 3

Although the Philippian faithful were unusually supportive of Paul, his enemies and detractors were active on the fringes. In chapter 3:2, 3, he turned the spotlight on them and attempted to weaken their claims by a terse review of his own Jewish roots. If these Judaizing hecklers suggested that true Jews could not be so blind as to accept the erroneous Christian story, Paul shredded that argument by outdoing them, showing that his Jewishness was more rigorous than their Jewishness. But nothing of that life compared with the "surpassing worth of knowing Christ Jesus my Lord" (8).

As we have seen already, Paul did not fear death, for he felt confident about his status with God. But he was very clear that his confidence did not rest on personal perfection (12, 13), but on the fact that Christ Jesus "has made me his own" (12). So his "straining forward" and "press[ing] on" (13, 14) were not a works-oriented struggle for perfection but were simply his way of expressing how he was working out his salvation each day, just as he had told them to do in chapter 2:12. It is in this respect that he could invite them to imitate his example of perseverance in faith (17).

Chapter 4

Paul concluded his letter with a series of practical instructions about Christian living that are unsurpassed in their simplicity and beauty. Every person on earth would like to have "no anxiety about anything" (6), and such peace can be attained by those who are willing to thankfully make known their requests to God. Regarding Christian standards of thought and practice, the admonition to think about the true and honorable and just and pure (8) is probably one of the most quoted texts in the Bible. Paul could be deep and complicated, or he could be simple and clear. In Philippians, he was mostly the latter.

Additional readings on chapter 14

1. Francis W. Beare, "The Epistle to the Ephesians" in *The Interpreter's Bible*, vol. 10, ed. George A. Buttrick (New York and Nashville: Abingdon, 1953).
2. _____.,*The Epistle to the Philippians* (New York: Harper and Row, 1959).
3. F. F. Bruce, *The Epistles to the Colossians, to Philemon, and to the Ephesians, The New International Commentary on the New Testament*, ed. F. F. Bruce (Grand Rapids, Mich.: Eerdmans, 1984).
4. John Knox, "The Epistle to Philemon" in *The Interpreter's Bible*, vol. 11, ed. George A. Buttrick (New York and Nashville: Abingdon, 1955).
5. G. Preston MacLeod, "The Epistle to the Colossians," in *The Interpreter's Bible*, vol. 11, ed. George A. Buttrick (New York and Nashville: Abingdon, 1955).
6. Jac. J. Muller, *The Epistles of Paul to the Philippians and to Philemon, The New International Commentary on the New Testament*, ed. N. B. Stonehouse (Grand Rapids, Mich.: Eerdmans, 1974).
7. J. A. Robinson, *St. Paul's Epistle to the Ephesians*, 2nd ed. (London: Macmillan, 1914).
8. Ernest F. Scott, *The Epistles of Paul to the Philippians and to Philemon, The New International Commentary on the New Testament*, ed. N. B. Stonehouse (Grand Rapids, Mich.: Eerdmans, 1974).
9. Ellen G. White, *The Acts of the Apostles*, pp. 453-484.
10. A. Skevington Wood, *Ephesians, The Expositor's Bible Commentary*, ed. Frank E. Gaebelein (Grand Rapids, Mich.: Zondervan, 1978).

Chapter
Sixteen

The Pastoral Epistles

1 and 2 Timothy, Titus

Paul was not exactly thought of as a family man, but his expressions of affection for Timothy are touching in their pathos. Timothy was the son Paul never had. It all began when Paul revisited Lystra on his second missionary journey. At that point he met a young man named Timothy, who was "well spoken of by the brethren at Lystra and Iconium" (Acts 16:2). Since Paul had visited these same towns on his first journey, it is conceivable that the two men met then, but that first visit had been a riot—literally. A group of Jews attempted to stone Paul's party at Iconium (Acts 14:5) and succeeded in doing so at Lystra (Acts 14:19), very nearly killing Paul. In all that excitement, it was difficult to recruit new help! Furthermore, at that point, Timothy may have been too young. But Paul's second visit to the area was more calm. As he looked forward to his coming missionary activities and sized up the youthful and committed Timothy, he quickly realized his value for the evangelistic team. Thus began a friendship that was to grow and strengthen until, after some eighteen years of shared joys and sorrows, the bond between them was like that between father and son. There is truly an emotional tug in Paul's words: "I have no one like him . . . as a son with a father he has served with me in the gospel" (Phil. 2:20-22).

Some have suggested that since Timothy's parents were not

both Jews (his father was a Greek, Acts 16:1), their marriage would have been considered illegal by Jewish law. Such a possibility puts a special meaning in Paul's statement, "My true child in the faith" (1 Tim. 1:2). Since some had insinuated nasty things about Timothy's natural birth, Paul vigorously asserted that there was no question about the genuineness of his spiritual birth—he is a "true child in the faith." Being part of a devoted family (2 Tim. 1:5) made him of special value for the ministry. Given his qualifications and his special bond with Paul, it is not surprising that Timothy was entrusted with the supervision of the Ephesus church (1 Tim. 1:3).

The Pastoral Epistles

The term *pastoral epistles* was first used for 1 and 2 Timothy and Titus in the eighteenth century. Since the short letters are made up of directives from an old missionary to young Christian workers, the term *pastorals* was so appropriate that it stuck. The variety of its counsel, coupled with its pastoral tone, makes 1 Timothy the most pastoral of the three letters. With its message of farewell, 2 Timothy is the least pastoral, with Titus falling between the two. These three short messages are the only Pauline letters written exclusively to one individual (even Philemon is also directed to Apphia, Archippus, and the church meeting in Philemon's house, Philem. 2).

While the style and vocabulary indicate that the three letters belong together, the contents suggest that 1 Timothy and Titus are most closely associated, while 2 Timothy stands apart. The objectives and procedures of 1 Timothy and Titus are the same—to offer practical instruction to the two men on how best to direct the churches committed to them. In contrast, 2 Timothy is the most personal of all Paul's letters as he reflects upon his own situation and anticipates his death in the very near future.

Historical setting

The historical setting of the "pastorals" poses a problem in that the events described don't fit into the history of Paul's life as found in Acts. For example, the account in Acts ends with Paul in Rome, under house arrest, but able to preach and teach "quite openly and unhindered" (Acts 28:31). Earlier, Luke recorded firsthand Paul's journey to that Roman imprisonment, and Timothy had been their traveling companion (Acts 20:4). Yet 1 Timothy 1:3, written after Acts, had Paul traveling alone through Macedonia, urging Timothy to remain at Ephesus. Nowhere does this situation (Paul in Macedonia, Timothy in Ephesus) fit into the travels of Paul and Timothy as recorded in Acts. Furthermore, in 2 Timothy 4:16 Paul referred to his "first defense" and how all his helpers had deserted him—which he hoped wouldn't be repeated at his upcoming second defense. Acts knows nothing of a second defense. There is likewise no reference in Acts to a ministry in Crete, where Titus was left in charge (Titus 1:5).

The common suggestion is that the Roman imprisonment mentioned in Acts 28:30 was not Paul's final imprisonment. If Paul had been martyred at that point, Luke surely would have mentioned it. Several early Christian writers implied that Paul was released. Church historian Roy J. Deferrari says:

> Paul is said, after having defended himself, to have set forth again upon the ministry of preaching, and to have entered the city (Rome) a second time, and to have ended his life by martyrdom. Whilst then a prisoner, he wrote the Second Epistle to Timothy, in which he both mentions his first defense, and his impending death (*Ecclesiastical History*, trans. Roy J. Deferrari [New York: Fathers of the Church, 1953], bk. 2, p. 123).

Where he traveled after his release is not certain. Earlier (Rom. 15:24) he had expressed hope that his journey to Rome would be a means of achieving the even greater goal of preaching in Spain, the perceived western limit of civilization. But there is no overwhelming evidence either in Scripture or early Christian literature that he ever reached Spain. Instead, near the end of his Roman imprisonment, he told Philemon (22), who was living in Colossae, to prepare a guest room, as he was planning to visit him in the near future.

Conceivably, after his two-year Roman imprisonment, conditions in the eastern churches were such that Paul felt constrained to visit them again rather than press on into new territory, so he abandoned or postponed his earlier plan to take the gospel to Spain. According to this hypothesis, his first Roman imprisonment (A.D. 61-63) was followed by a tour of teaching and nurturing believers in regions previously visited (A.D. 64-66), during which time he wrote 1 Timothy and Titus. He was then recaptured as part of the Neronian persecutions, which were precipitated by the great fire in Rome in A.D. 64 and Nero's subsequent attempt to make scapegoats of the Christians. Following Paul's final arrest (A.D. 66), he wrote 2 Timothy, just prior to his execution (2 Tim. 4:6).

Authorship

There has been considerable debate about the Pauline authorship of the pastoral epistles. Two of the major objections have been that the church organization reflected in the pastorals is too advanced for them to have been written in the first century, and the vocabulary of the pastorals is quite different from that of the other Pauline epistles.

The first objection is based on use of the terms *elder*, *bishop*, and *deacon*. The implication seems to be that these terms mean the same things in the pastorals that they meant in the second and third centuries—a hierarchy of church offices with *elder* at the top and *deacon* at the bottom. However, Titus 1:5, 7 shows that the terms *elder* and *bishop* were used interchangeably. Also, in Philippians, a letter widely accepted as Pauline, the apostle mentioned both bishops and deacons (1:1). Moreover, the organization was quite primitive, as elders were to be appointed in every community (Titus 1:5), and all elders were equal in authority. In fact, it seems that references in the pastoral epistles to various church offices and rituals do not represent a significant advance or development of those offices, which would necessitate a second- or third-century date. The organization described in the pastorals is really quite simple and therefore consistent with both an early date and Pauline authorship.

The second objection rests on the fact that these three short letters contain 131 words that occur elsewhere in the New Testament but not in Pauline material and an additional 175 words that occur nowhere else in the New Testament (P. N. Harrison, *The Problem of the Pastoral Epistles* [London: Oxford University Press, 1921], pp. 20, 21). Paul did use secretaries in the writing and delivering of his letters, so unless he actually dictated his material verbatim, which seems unlikely, the vocabulary of the secretary would show up in the letter. When this idea is combined with the fact that a large number of words common to Luke/Acts and the pastorals are found nowhere else in the New Testament, the intriguing possibility arises that Luke was Paul's secretary. In addition, a change of subject matter often required a change of vocabulary, and this could account for many of the unique words.

Occasion and purpose of 1 Timothy and Titus

Given their close personal relationship, Paul's first letter to Timothy is surprising. One might expect the old warrior to spend some time reminiscing about the days gone by, but instead he plunged almost immediately into a blunt warning about false teachings that seemed to be gaining ground. Paul was not occupied with presenting the gospel in an evangelistic way so much as he was in calling Timothy and the church to remember and live up to what they had already heard. He was not planting a new crop, but hoeing the weeds out of the old one. Some had already departed from the faith, he said, but Timothy was to concern himself with the well-being of the church and thus pray for all men, especially those in high positions who might have some influence over the quiet, peaceable life that Christians are called upon to lead (2:2). Paul went on to give directions on how best to deal with a variety of groups within the church—women, elders, bishops, deacons, and widows. He concluded with a moving personal appeal to Timothy to remain faithful and not fall away like others had done.

While considerably shorter, Titus is very similar to 1 Timothy. Paul began by reminding Titus of his commission to "amend what was defective" (1:5) and followed with many of the same instructions for bishops and church leaders that he had given to Timothy. He concluded with some brief greetings and an appeal to try to meet him in Nicopolis.

Occasion and purpose of 2 Timothy

There is a note of acute sadness about Paul's second letter to Timothy. His missionary journeys were now history, and he had tasted freedom for the last time. Fortunately, he had trained younger men to take over the work. Titus in Crete, Carpus in Troas, and Crescens in Galatia. The imminence of the executioner's sword (2 Tim. 4:6) had impressed upon him that his human relationships were about to end. But the loneliness that here oppressed him was the abandonment by fellow workers at a time when he needed to feel their support. "Demas, in love with this present world, has deserted me" (4:10). Poignant words! In addition, Paul felt burdened with the growing apprehension that, for some members, the future held "times of stress" (3:1) from men "who oppose the truth" (3:8).

This, then, is one of Paul's most personal and poignant letters. From his death cell he was bidding farewell to one who was most like the son he never had. But in spite of his personal suffering, Paul was not awash in self-pity. In fact, he directed attention to his difficulties only to forearm young Timothy for similar pains that were all too soon to come upon him. Thus, Paul's primary purpose in this letter was to comfort and sustain Timothy in the face of imminent persecution (note the repeated phrase, "Take your share in suffering"—1:8, 2:3; and the frequent references to persecution and endurance). But along with that theme, Paul also warned Timothy about coming heresies and offered suggestions about how he should deal with them. The implication of the letter seems clear: "Therefore, Timothy [and all future Timothys], you too can face an uncertain future with confidence, for the crown of righteousness will be awarded not only to me, but also to you, and to all who keep the faith and love his appearing" (4:8, author's paraphrase).

1 Timothy

Chapter 1—When opposition mounts, hold fast the faith

The term *Bible doctrine* is often thought of as Christian teachings that have been organized into well-defined topics, usually with a series of supporting texts. When Paul cautioned Timothy about a "different doctrine," some interpreters conclude that that kind of instruction would make sense only after Christian teaching had had a couple of centuries to gel into organized subjects. But in chapter 1:5 Paul indicated that his idea of doctrine was quite simple: love from a pure heart, a good conscience, and sincere faith. While this was not all he had to say about Christian teaching and practice, his practical counsels here were hardly the kind of systematic theology that would take years to codify.

Admittedly, Paul was quite explicit in what he taught and very forthright in stating what he expected from believers, so the notion of what was considered "orthodox" or "heretical" would not take long to develop. It would certainly not take decades, let alone centuries, as some have suggested. The fact is that when Paul scorned various false teachings, his language was quite vague, as he warned about "myths and endless genealogies," "speculations" (4), and a general quarrelsomeness. Such terms are not precise enough to refer to the heretical systems of belief that were typical of the second or third centuries. In other words, his language was perfectly consistent with conditions in first-century Christianity. He seems to have felt no need to further define either his "orthodoxy" or the "heresy" that threatened, since Timothy apparently knew what he was referring to.

Misunderstanding the function of law has been a problem for Christians from Paul's day to ours. In verses 8-11 the exact nature of law abuse is not clear, but it sounds like legalism on the one hand (9) and antinomianism (10, 11) on the other. Thus, some of the Christians under Timothy's care had regressed to an experience of law domination from which the "just" (9) had been set free, and others were living in flagrant disobedience and immorality, as if the Christian life had no responsibility. Paul had already made it clear that after the law has performed its function of pointing out sin (Rom. 3:20) and the believer has been freed by Christ from its condemnation, its function as an objective guide becomes more and more inward, as Christ, the Author of the law, increasingly dominates the Christian's life and interests. But apparently some in Ephesus were continuing to teach the "letter of the law" to Christians (7-9).

Paul's dogmatic tone called for a statement of credentials, so verses 12-17 reminded his readers of his own checkered past and of the power of that grace which had turned his life around. The change in his life had been brought about, not by a deeper insight into the meaning of the law, but by the mercy of the "King of ages," to whom Paul would give honor and glory forever (17).

Chapter 2—Instructions for public worship

Christians may sometimes debate the meaning and method of intercessory prayer, but they cannot debate the instruction to pray. For example, in verses 2:1, 2 Paul clearly taught the need for prayer on behalf of the many officials who were influential in keeping the peace so the Christian gospel could advance. As he pondered the impact of the gospel message, Paul offered in verses 5, 6 a powerful summary statement about that gospel that beautifully incorporates the Old Testament stress on monotheism and the Christian message of redemption. His assertion that "there is one God" is the kernel of Judaism, while his addition that there is "one mediator between God and men, the man Christ Jesus" is the gospel condensed. These two verses comprise one of the most powerful condensations in the New Testament.

What follows in verses 8-15 is one of the more controversial Pauline passages. With the steady advance in the status of women in the Western world, Paul's appeals for an orderly worship service in which the men are in harmony and the women are silent and submissive have become more and more troublesome. But it is important to understand what Paul was *not* saying as well as what he was saying. He was not forbidding women to teach in all circumstances. In Titus 2:3 he admonished the older women to teach the younger ones, and elsewhere he approved the work of certain women teachers (Acts 18:26; Phil. 4:3). When, in verse 12, he said that he permitted no women to teach, he continued with "or to have authority over men." This is a significant phrase. In other words, as Paul sized up the situation in the Ephesus church, he saw women occupying an *official* teaching capacity in the church, in effect, upstaging men in general and husbands in particular.

The Jews made a division in their synagogues, segregated the sexes, and allowed no woman to have an active role in the service. But apparently the Christian gospel had brought a sense of liberation to women that, in Corinth, threatened to get out of hand and bring reproach upon the church. Paul felt a deep concern about those women in Ephesus who were "gadding about . . . gossips and busybodies, saying what they should not" (5:13). In 5:15 he even added that "some have . . . strayed after Satan." Consequently, because of the behavior of the Ephesian women, Paul felt constrained to spell out some rules by which Timothy could keep order in the public service of worship.

The difficulty with the present passage is the reasoning behind Paul's prohibition. The rationale for Paul's directives about submissive women comes from the Creation story and therefore seems to reach far beyond a first-century Ephesus application. For example, the first reason he gave for the submissive position of women was the chronological order of creation. Because Adam was created first, he had a more authoritative role than Eve (13). However, Paul's own testimony on this point was divided, for in 1 Corinthians 11:11, 12, he added that "in the Lord woman is not independent of man nor man of woman, for as woman was made from man, so man is now born of woman." The leveling, equalizing effect of that statement is quite instructive.

But Paul's second reason for the submissive role of women is even more difficult, for he next asserted that Eve was deceived, while Adam was not (14). Paul was not suggesting that Adam was innocent. In fact, in his theological discussion about the entrance of sin into the world (Rom. 5:12), he never even mentioned Eve. If anything, Adam's sinning in the light of knowledge made his guilt greater than Eve's. But in Paul's mind, the issue was not guilt but gullibility. Apparently he was saying that one who is easily led astray should not be entrusted with the responsibility involved in being a teacher. But why did Paul connect Eve with the Christian women in his day? The answer lies in the Hebrew concept of solidarity. In this regard, Eve is the symbol and embodiment of all women, whose example all women will inexorably follow. Where she is weak, all her female offspring will likewise be weak. But if susceptibility to temptation is not a more female than male trait, what can we say about Paul's reasoning here?

It was common practice for Bible writers to make varied applications of Old Testament texts, some of which had little to do with the original context. In Romans 10:15 Paul made very different use of the wording of Isaiah 52:7 than Isaiah had originally intended. Similarly, in Romans 10:18, he quoted Psalm 19 but applied it to the spread of the gospel by the New Testament evangelists, whereas the original statement referred to the "testimony" of the heavenly bodies. Similar examples are numerous. Yet this in no way detracts from Paul or his inspiration. It is perfectly legitimate for an inspired writer to make new applications of words or principles that appeared earlier in a much different context. And while the new application also contains a divine imperative, that imperative may be more appropriate to one age than to another.

Applying all this to the passage at hand might work like this. The problem of liberated Christian women bringing reproach upon the Ephesus church needed to be corrected quickly and decisively. As Paul thought and reasoned, he saw in the Creation story points of logic that would help to enforce his imperative. Perhaps he was doing just what Jesus did with the parable of the rich man and Lazarus in Luke 16, when He "used the prevailing opinion [method of reasoning] to convey the idea He wished to make prominent" (Ellen White, *Christ's Object Lessons* [Hagerstown, Md: Review and Herald, 1941], p. 263).

Whatever conclusion we reach about Paul's passage, we must allow him a certain latitude in his reasoning process and interpret his words carefully and prayerfully. In the context of 1 Timothy it is clear that Paul was using the incident of Eve as an example of female weakness to press his point about impropriety upon the Ephesian women. But we must be very cautious about lifting this out of its historical and social context and turning it into a universal absolute.

The final difficulty of the passage is the meaning of the clause, "Woman will be saved through bearing children" (15). Various interpretations have been advanced, including the suggestion that all women will be saved who bear children. Another view is that women will be saved because a woman bore the Christ Child. But the most reasonable interpretation seems to be that the verb *save* should be taken in a spiritual sense, and childbearing is used here as a general reference to an attitude of submission to the divinely appointed role and function for women. In other words, when a woman humbly fits into her God-given role, and of course maintains faith, love, and holiness (15), she will be saved. The way of salvation is the way of submission, not an arrogant flaunting of newly discovered freedoms. Such arrogance among the Ephesian women cast a bad light on the fledgling Christian movement and also killed that spirit of humility so necessary to the women's future salvation. This advice, of course, applies equally to men, even though Paul did not say so.

Chapter 3—Qualifications for bishops and deacons

Paul listed the qualifications for bishops and deacons separately (1-7, 8-13), thus implying that they represented two different offices in the early church. But the lists are so similar that it is impossible to determine how the offices differed. The word Paul used for *bishop* meant "overseer," and he even seems to interchange it with *elder* (Titus 1:6, 7). From Acts 20:17, 18 it appears that there could have been several bishops/elders in each local church, which does some violence to the idea that a bishop was the most important figure in each local church structure. Thus, the term *overseer* may be a more precise description, and one less weighted with ecclesiastical overtones. While comment could be made about each of the various qualifications for bishops and deacons, most of them are quite transparent.

One that has sparked some discussion is "husband of one wife," a qualification for both bishop and deacon. This statement, coupled with certain ascetic influences, gave rise to the practice of clerical celibacy, but such an interpretation goes beyond the intent of the passage. Even the translation "married only once" is not supported by the original phrase. Most expositors believe Paul simply meant that church leaders must be monogamous and totally faithful.

Chapter 4—Various instructions to Timothy

When Paul felt the gospel was being in any sense distorted, he had no burden to be temperate in his language. Thus "hypocritical liars with seared consciences" may strike our pampered ears as more than a little blunt, but in Paul's mind, protection of the gospel was at stake, and verbal niceties had to give way. Presumably, these ascetics, who, among other prohibitions, were "forbid[ding] to marry," knew better, but had deliberately forsaken the simple gospel. Their demands are reminiscent of those that afflicted the Colossian church and may well have arisen out of the same spirit-matter dualism that held all physical pleasure to be sin.

Paul's reference to physical fitness in verse 8 is brief but instructive. He granted its value, but in the process showed that there is a higher priority. Physical discipline is good, but gives value only to this life, while spiritual discipline benefits this life as well the life to come. Then in verses 11-16 he specified several pastoral responsibilities that he wanted Timothy to give attention to. Paul's reference to Timothy's youth is relative, for Timothy was probably in his mid-thirties. But it appears that, in terms of his giving counsel and directing the activities of the church, some looked upon his age as a handicap.

Chapter 5—Counsel regarding various groups

The warmth and tenderness in 5:1, 2 form a stark contrast to the way Paul began chapter 4. Here he exhorted Timothy to regard the members as he would members of a family, with compassion for the elders and propriety for the younger females. In verses 3-16, he devoted special attention to the widows, counseling tender care but also warning that they were prone to become gossips and busybodies.

"Respect for one's elders" was more than a chiché for Paul. While the term often meant simply an older person, Paul clearly used it in a technical sense of "elder of the church" in 5:17, 19. In this passage, Paul instructed Timothy to treat the elders with honor and respect and to beware of stories that put them in a bad light (19). Paul was not the kind of man to foster blind loyalty or superstitious honor. Rather, it is apparent that he advocated genuine respect for men of character.

Verse 23 has been subject to much discussion, since total abstinence from alcoholic drinks has been the position of many conservative Christian groups, and this verse seems to suggest otherwise. In all fairness, it must be admitted that the Greek word for *wine*, by itself, does not indicate the presence or absence of alcoholic content. The word is used in the Septuagint (Greek translation of the Old Testament) for the unfermented juice of the grape, but it is also used in passages where fermentation had taken place. But Paul was referring to a medicinal use of wine, which is not inconsistent with the cautions against strong drink that are scattered throughout the rest of Scripture. The fermented wine in Paul's day was quite weak, and we know that the Jews often diluted it further with water. If that is the nature of the wine referred to here, and if Paul was suggesting a very limited, medicinal use, it would be faulty interpretation to find in this verse an excuse for recreational or social drinking.

Chapter 6—Counsel to Christian slaves and closing admonitions

If, as some have said, the slaves of the Roman Empire outnumbered the freemen by as many as three to one, it is not surprising that Paul several times gave counsel to the Christians among them. Whether their masters were unbelievers or believers, Christian slaves were to remember that their example of consistent Christian living rebounded upon the name and reputation of their true Master, Jesus Christ.

In his closing counsels, Paul warned the believers to avoid the foolish controversies that were prevalent and to shun the love of material things. The Christian calling is to higher values—godliness, faith, and love (11, 12).

Titus

Titus is a very small package, but of course, precious gems often come packaged that way. Though very short, it merits our attention for a couple of reasons. First, it may well have been the only letter from Paul to Titus, as it is in the form of a compact summary, and summaries often make important reading. Second, it was written very late in Paul's life and thus takes on the urgency and intensity of a farewell message. In a last will and testament, people try hard to avoid trivialities.

Titus had been a former traveling companion and co-laborer with Paul, and in the process had become, like Timothy, a kind of godson ("my true child in a common faith," 1:4). Yet the letter has more than affectionate reminiscences. Even a casual glance catches such words as *debauchery, dissipation, undisciplined, arrogant, drunken,* and *slanderous.* It appears that the believers on the island of Crete needed help with some very practical aspects of Christian living. In fact, in these three short chapters, the term for Christian works occurs eight times. Once again, it is clear that Paul, the great architect of righteousness by faith, did not slight the practical aspects of Christian living.

While the bulk of the letter is composed of the dos and don'ts of Christian responsibility, Paul put together a beautiful summation in 2:11-14. With no ambiguity, he asserted that the grace of God impels us to renounce evil and live godly lives while we await Christ's return. Or, as he reiterated in verse 14, Christ has purified for Himself people who then are "zealous for good deeds." There is no legalism in Christian works that spring from His purifying grace.

2 Timothy

Chapter 1—Joys and sorrows of being called to minister

Timothy, like all Christians, owed his spiritual life to influences outside of himself. Paul reminded him of his spiritual heritage by referring to the influence of his mother and grandmother (5) and the "gift of God" within that was the result of Paul's ministry on his behalf (6). Still, whatever has come to us from others is to be nurtured, "rekindled" every day. Not only that, but the whole ongoing experience may well take place in the midst of suffering, which is an integral part of ministering in the name of Jesus (8-14). However, the Christian who is willing to make that commitment will, even now, participate in the life and immortality brought to light in the gospel (10).

So often Paul comes across as the tireless worker, the iron man who knows no defeat or discouragement, who either wins his hearers for Christ or walks away in triumphant disgust if they will not be moved. But in this short letter, more than any other, Paul's personal feelings show through, and they are normal, sensitive, often hurting feelings. Thus, he speaks plainly of his hurt over those who have abandoned him and his gratitude for those few who have remained faithful (1:15-18; 4:9-18). Human companionship was always important, but it took on even greater meaning as his life neared its close.

Chapter 2—Discipline and suffering will finally be rewarded

Apparently Timothy and the other believers in Ephesus had to live their Christianity in the face of ridicule and opposition. Such a prospect is never pleasant, but Paul assured them that hardship and discipline are the hallmarks of the Christian life. He made his point by the analogies of the soldier, the athlete, and the farmer (3-6). Paul's message comes clearly to focus in verses 11-13, where he asserted that the Christian may have to endure suffering and may even be called upon to give up his life, but "if we endure, we shall also reign with him" (12). He added the analogy of his own example of suffering, reminding them that he was once again "wearing fetters" (9) but was willing to endure anything "for the sake of the elect" (10). Throughout the remainder of the chapter he warned about the dangers of foolish controversies, and he cited two examples—Hymenaeus and Philetus (17), who were casualties of some of the false teachings that were circulating.

Chapter 3—Heresy and suffering will increase, but the Scriptures are a safeguard

The future for the Ephesian Christians sounded rather grim as Paul listed the corrupt attitudes and practices that would constantly threaten to invade them (1-9). But as he did in chapter 1, he again reminded the members that opposition, persecution, and heresy are to be expected. But there is a defense: Remember what you have learned and who taught you. Also, if you make the effort, the sacred writings "are able to instruct you" (15). Only with their help can the people of God be "complete, equipped for every good work" (17).

Chapter 4—Paul's final charge and testimony

Parting words are never frivolous, especially when the farewell is final and the friendship tight. Such is the situation in 2 Timothy 4. In the first five verses, Paul seems to measure his words much more carefully than usual, as he charged Timothy to put his every effort into the proclamation of the gospel, no matter what the personal cost. Then, with emotion clearly showing, Paul reminded Timothy that he would no longer be able to look to Paul to direct him, for he, Paul, was about to be sacrificed. Paul was not so much looking for sympathy as he was alerting Timothy to his need to shoulder the mantle of leadership after the manner of Paul. His final testimony is not arrogant but is filled with confidence that because he had kept faith in his Lord, his crown of righteousness was assured. Furthermore, the same assurance can be experienced by all "who have loved his appearing" (8).

Paul's confident testimony was made even more meaningful as he revealed in verses 9-18 that his physical surroundings were very trying. Except for Luke, his friends had deserted him, and he felt the need for human companionship. Nevertheless, his final word was one of confidence that the same Lord who had rescued him so many times before will "save me for his heavenly kingdom" (18).

What assurance, what confidence, what peace!

Throughout his life and ministry, Paul's friends seemed few and his enemies numberless. But while he cherished companionship, his passion for the gospel and its advance so dominated his time and efforts that, although he died virtually alone, it was not in defeat. He had been instrumental in spreading the exciting news about Jesus from the narrow boundaries of Palestine to the major cities of Asia Minor, Macedonia, Greece, and now Italy. His early enemies would have been incensed had they known how prophetic was their derision about "these men who have turned the world upside down" (Acts 17:6). Paul died in triumph, for the life-changing, world-changing message was well on its way.

Additional readings on chapter 15

1. William Barclay, *The Letters to Timothy, Titus and Philemon*, The Daily Study Bible (Philadelphia: Westminster, 1975).
2. Ralph Earle, *1, 2 Timothy, The Expositor's Bible Commentary*, ed. Frank E. Gaebelein (Grand Rapids, Mich.: Zondervan, 1978).
3. Fred Gealy and Morgan P. Noyes, "The First and Second Epistles to Timothy and the Epistle to Titus," *The Interpreter's Bible* (New York and Nashville: Abingdon, 1955).
4. Donald Guthrie, *The Pastoral Epistles*, Tyndale Bible Commentary (Grand Rapids, Mich.: Eerdmans, 1957).
5. D. Edmond Hiebert, *Titus and Philemon*, in Everyman's Bible Commentary (Grand Rapids, Mich.: Zondervan, 1978).
6. Ellen G. White, *The Acts of the Apostles*, pp. 489-513.